FLORIDA STATE
UNIVERSITY LIBRARIES

DEC 23 1997

TALLAHASSEE, FLORIDA

Davai, Davai!

Davai, Davai!

Memoir of a German Prisoner of World War II in the Soviet Union

A. D. Hans Schuetz

McFarland & Company, Inc., Publishers
Jefferson, North Carolina, and London

"Davai, Davai!"— Russian for "Move along! Get going!"

Sketches by Melanie D. Nuchols

British Library Cataloguing-in-Publication data are available

Library of Congress Cataloguing-in-Publication Data

Schuetz, A. D. Hans, 1916–
    Davai, davai! : memoir of a German prisoner of World War II in the Soviet Union / A. D. Hans Schuetz.
    p.   cm.
    Includes index.
    ISBN 0-7864-0402-7 (library binding : 50# alkaline paper) ∞
    1. Schuetz, A. D. Hans, 1916–   . 2. World War, 1939–1945 — Prisoners and prisons, Soviet. 3. World War, 1939–1945 — Personal narratives, German. 4. Prisoners of war — Soviet Union — Biography. I. Title.
D805.S65S38   1997
940.54'7247 — dc21   97-26242
                                                                                                  CIP

©1997 A. D. Hans Schuetz. All rights reserved

No part of this book, specifically including the table of contents and index, may be reproduced or transmitted in any form or by any means, electronic or mechanical, including photocopying or recording, or by any information storage and retrieval system, without permission in writing from the publisher.

Manufactured in the United States of America

McFarland & Company, Inc., Publishers
  Box 611, Jefferson, North Carolina 28640

Acknowledgments

THIS BOOK IS WRITTEN in memory of our younger son, Michael Manfred Schuetz, and for our only two grandsons, Christopher H. Schuetz and Kevin M. Schuetz. I always wanted to write down my experiences for my sons, and later for my grandsons, but I never got around to it. After retirement from my construction company, I found time and again had the urge to write about what I had experienced in World War II.

I want to thank Jim Petrinas for his assistance in editing the early part of the book and Katherine Tyler for her advice, editing, and typing and retyping. Inna Malyshev and Alex Purinsh were very helpful with the spelling of the Russian words. Bill Taylor spent many hours editing a later draft.

I am much obliged to Professor Horst Richardson from Colorado College in Colorado Springs and his wife, Helen, for their encouragement and proofreading to help complete the job.

After reading the manuscript, Melanie Nuchols caught the spirit well in creating the drawings.

Many thanks go to my late wife, Annemarie, for her understanding and support during those many hours I spent writing the manuscript.

Above all, I am grateful for the Grace of God, which brought me into the situation, carried me through step by step, and in 1951 brought me safely with my family to the land of my dreams and desire, the United States of America.

I am convinced that God always works out His purpose, even if we cannot understand it at the time it happens.

Contents

Prologue	1
The End at Last	5
Last Hope. Feast. The Unexpected. Exodus. The Party Is Over	
An End and a Beginning	13
"Davai, Uri!" Not Given but Taken. Close Call. A Little White Bag. Seek and Ye Shall Find. Interrogation	
Marching to a Different Drummer	20
A Long Walk. Wasted Effort. Service: Hospital Style. End of the Trail! Or…?	
It Is Finished!	25
Tears. Rolling via Railroad. Boxed In. An Expensive Hole	
A Continent Divided	31
Breslau	
Train to Somewhere	33
Going East. Just a Break, but a Blessing	
Caucasus	35
Coat Collection. Memories. Uncertain Directions	
Saratov (Zorotov)	43
Arrival. The Garden of Eden. "Saratov Special." Banja. No Round Trip. Night Visitors. Home Sweet Home. But Here Are the Facts. Who Comes to Dinner Tonight? Talk About It. Three Left Over. Nothing to Do. Günther. "Budit" (It Will Be). One "Budit" Turned into Reality. Hot Soup	
The Sawmill	53
A Blessing. The First Job Assignment. The Menu. Improvements. Love Story. It Comes, It Goes. Cranking Up the Mill. Midnight Dreams. A Pleasant Visitor. Homestead. Franz. Rudi	

Contents

The Yeast Plant   61
A New Job. Davai Brigadier. On the Road. Vodka. The Hungarians. Borscht

Night Shift   66
"Chisty, Chisty." Postcard. Christmas Cookies. Chai. With My Bare Hands. A Fill-In. The Bath

In Between Jobs   74
The Honey Wagon. One Escapes. Too Much. Buttocks Show. Downtown. Music of the Spheres. Half and Half

Tannery   81
Another New Job. Talon Budit. Russian Prisoners of War. Just a Spoon. Tsap-Tsarap. The Escapee Returns. Chess. Far, Far Away. Our Real Enemy. One Who Really Suffered. Never Again. Mail Arrived. Little Ferocious Enemies. No More Suffering. Promises to Live On. Plans for the Winter. Listless and Unresponsive

The Hospital   98
Ambulance Service. A Lukewarm Welcome. Next? A Piece of Bacon? After-Effects. Rumors, Blessed Rumors. Touching Only. Standing Transport

Atkarsk!   104
Born Again. House I and House II. Little White Mice. Sickroom. Heating Systems. Haven't Learned Yet. House II. Three Under Three. With the Help of the Sun. Back in Paradise. A Message to Home. Changing of the Guard. Pleasant Visitors. Valkyrie

Another World   112
Night Visits. The Key to Going Home. My View. The Act of Providence. Carvers' Corner. Going Home? Called Back. The Promise

Engels   118
Return to Reality. First Impression. Four-Hour Shifts. Ready to Work. On-the-Job Training. Bookkeeping. Doomed to Rot. Moral Armament. Music in the Camp. Camp Production. Winter Comes. St. Nick's Warm-up. Blackboards. Christmas. The Restroom

The Conference   129
Walking on Water. Moment of Silence. The Lucky Ones. Slow Return. Fast-Food Service

There and Here   135
Mystery News. Compassion. Misha

The Fence   138
The Preparation. A Commission. Sounds. Happiness Is How You Look at Things. An Argument. Rumors. Downtown Engels. "Souper" or Dinner. Reminiscence. Movie. The Way Home. Action and Reaction. Exodus

Contents   ix

Camp I   148
  Return to Where It Began. Brigadier "Nyet." Specialist. Sawmill. Youth Leader. Out. Meeting Again. A Visitor. Buttocks Parade. A Family Picture

Going West   154
  First Class: Straw Bedding and Doors Open. Halt. Final End of the Wide Track. Partir C'est Mourir un Peu. Bells Are Ringing

Epilogue   161
Glossary   163
Index   167

Prologue

COULD THIS BE the same city, Berlin? It was always a city with a pulsing life force, cultural events, world renown. Visitors came to Berlin from all over the world, for business or pleasure, to experience this vast metropolis.

The many parks and the tree-lined streets and avenues gave a special beauty to Berlin. In early summer one could enjoy the fragrance of the blossoms of the linden trees facing some of the streets. They were pleasant memories, but how long ago? Had this terrible war really been going on for over five and a half years?

The Berliners are a special type of people. They are well known for their sense of humor, short and to the point, that carried them through the terrors that occurred in the city. As the war progressed, their humor turned into silence.

The people got used to blackouts all over occupied Europe (except for Switzerland and Sweden, neutral countries that kept their lights on and tried to ignore the war). During the time of full moon, nature gave light that street lights could no longer provide and made it easier to get around at night. On new moon nights familiar buildings, monuments, street corners, and squares faded in a strange shade of darkness. On some occasions, when the sky was clear, one could see stars shining down on the city just like in peacetime. In former times it would have been called romantic. I had almost forgotten what romance meant. It was all so long ago.

What had happened? Berlin was in ruins. Street by street, whole sectors of this once proud and beautiful city were nothing but ashes and rubble. Here and there the four walls of an apartment building were still standing, but the roof structure and the floors were a pile of ashes resting in the basement. The holes of windows and doorways gazed out into the black of the night. There was once life behind those walls — families living, kids growing up, children laughing, hope, and plans being made for a brighter future. All that was gone now. All gone!

Amazingly, people still walked the city streets. Everyone had lost loved ones either in the battlefields of Europe or in the destruction of German cities. Minds were dulled by the visible destruction. People felt betrayed. Hope was gone. Hope for what? What about the promises? The never-revealed miracle weapons? The last great deployment? More lies?

The bombings at night from the British airplanes and American airplanes by day had destroyed Berlin. Göring, the Air Field Marshall, had promised: "Never will there be any enemy airplanes over Berlin!"

He must not have told the British and the Americans. Göring, a child in a man's body, liked to play in uniforms and loved to dress up like a military prima donna.

Worse than Göring was the minister of enlightenment and propaganda, Joseph Goebbels, agitating the masses to defend the homeland with pitchforks and sticks, the inventor of the "Total War"—whatever that meant. Wasn't the war total enough after five and a half years of destruction to our cities and people?

Above all, there was Hitler—the self-styled "Führer" of the German nation, the self-proclaimed commander-in-chief who did not have any training in war tactics or knowledge of how to lead troops. How little the people really had known about that man! He had risen to the rank of private first class during World War I. That was the extent of his experience in commanding an army. Hitler had been rejected from an architectural school in Vienna. Had he ever held a job? He wrote *Mein Kampf* in prison after a failed revolt in Munich. He fooled a lot of people: diplomats, writers, businessmen, journalists, generals, and the easiest of all, the German people.

In 1932 Hitler lost the election for president to Hindenburg, who appointed Hitler as chancellor in January of 1933—the last legal action according to the law of the German Republic. On the same day as the death of president Hindenburg in August 1934, Hitler took over the office of president and combined both branches under his authority without election. That opened the door to absolute power and terror under the Nazi Party and its organizations and to persecution of the Jews and the German intelligensia. Those who stood up against Hitler and his terrifying regime were hunted down.

After he built the Wehrmacht, Hitler ordered his troops to occupy the Rhineland, the west bank of the Rhine River bordering France. He built the west wall and put heavy armament in concrete bunkers along the French border for protection. Did he fear an attack by France? There was no action from France or Great Britain, the only balancing powers in Europe in those days. However, the west wall came in very handy in 1940 as a base to attack France.

Early in 1938 he "liberated" Austria and brought that nation under Nazi terror. There was no response from the West! A year later he annexed the Sudetenland, part of Czechoslovakia. Great Britain intervened. Foreign Minister Chamberlain from England came to Munich to protest, but gave in since this was to be Hitler's last demand for territories in Europe. Shortly after that Hitler sent an ultimatum to the government of Czechoslovakia to surrender and become a "German Protectorate." If not, Prague, the capital, would be bombed the next day. Persecution of the Jews and destroying any opposition became the pattern for any country Hitler took over.

Prologue

Czechoslovakia yielded to Hitler. Terror followed diplomacy. In 1939 Hitler felt so strong that he overran Poland, and he later occupied Denmark, Norway, and the Balkan States. Doesn't the distribution of food ration coupons during the first days of the beginning of the war prove the true fact that a war had been planned long in advance? With the Blitzkrieg he sacked the Netherlands, Belgium, and France, following the same tactics of oppression. His surprise attacks had worked for a while.

But now, in the spring of 1945, what had Hitler accomplished? The Americans were ready to cross the Elbe River; the Russians were knocking on the gates of Berlin. Germany was occupied, the people demoralized, hopeless. Was Hitler still unable to see what he had done to his "own" people? In truth, he was not even German. He was imported from Austria — but to other nations he was German.

April 20, 1945, would be Hitler's birthday, but there would be no parades (he loved parades). There would be no troop reviews (there were no troops available). It would be a day of despair. Will he curse the day of his birth, or will he blame everyone around him, including the capitalistic enemies, for the terrible destruction he brought not only to Germany but to most parts of Europe?

Hitler and his cohorts had brought Germany to the brink of final destruction. The war around Berlin would last only days, maybe hours. Hitler had to know that if he was captured he would be brought before a military tribunal to be charged, convicted, and sentenced to death for the sins he had committed against the human race. Or would he attempt to escape his fate, as well as cheat the millions of tortured victims — dead and alive — one last time by committing suicide?

* * *

This is his hell: On a wide open, flat plane seemingly reaching to infinity — no banners, no flags or adoring people, no columns of marching troops — Hitler, without his usual entourage, stands alone. A row of human beings can be seen in the distance. In single file, they walk slowly, silently toward Hitler. As they come closer they can be identified as corpses — bloodied, mutilated, starved, and filthy — millions of people, killed as a result of Hitler's actions or orders. One by one they file past. Their vacant, expressionless, dead eyes stare at nothing. Hitler faces them, his left hand pressed against his belly button. His right arm stretched out in the famous "Heil, Hitler" greeting, he stands naked and exposed as he reviews the parade of bodies dragging past one by one, visible in the distance as far as the eye can see.

The light on this unearthly scene never varies. It has a diffused, artificially yellow glow. As "night" comes, Hitler finds himself in a round concrete enclosure perhaps ten feet in diameter — no doors, no windows. A bright light shines harshly from the ceiling. Hitler is fully dressed in his black pants, black shoes, brown shirt and tie and his well-known "baby-shit" colored jacket and famous cap.

In the middle of the room stands his beloved desk chair, lavishly decorated with the insignia of the Third Reich and the swastika. Hitler moves over and sits down. The chair collapses under his weight, seemingly made of a rubberlike material. He ends up on the floor. When Hitler rolls off, it springs back to its original shape. He attempts once more to sit on the chair with the same results. He crawls over to sit on the floor with his back against the concrete wall. From an unseen loudspeaker comes his own voice giving speeches, interrupted by readings from *Mein Kampf*.

"Morning" arrives and Hitler stands again on the parade ground to review the endless procession of corpses.

* * *

Finally, Hitler harvests the fruit of his thinking, his ideology, his action, and his orders by listening to his own speeches and reviewing the endless line of corpses forever and ever. Is this the prologue to hell?

The End at Last

Last Hope Yes, I heard it. I didn't want to, but I did. There, it came closer that time.

Every morning it was the same routine: the sound of the back of the knuckle against the door.

"*Aufstehen!*" (Get up!). It was the voice of the corporal on duty.

Three doors away; no, four? The sound of the heels of the boots, *click, click* ... the knock on the door:

"*Aufstehen.*"

The gentle greeting was now at my door. That ritual of awakening into reality was the privilege of the instructors. It brought us back from wherever we were with our thoughts and dreams or our other escapes from reality. My nature made it possible for me to always wake immediately and jump out of bed. I was usually one of the first in the washroom with a fresh, "*Guten Morgen*" (Good morning).

I barely heard the mumble of a dreary voice: "What's so good about it?"

I answered: "We're at least one day closer to the victory."

No answer came. In the dim light of the washroom I could not see the expression on the faces of those who were already in the process of their morning toilette.

The almost five and a half years of the war had taught me to shave without a mirror and even in the darkness of the morning. There was still a little piece of shaving soap left. It wouldn't last much longer. But every morning the scent lifted me up out of the gray, monotonous, hopeless routine of the daily duties that confronted me.

No hot shower, but there was plenty of fresh, cold running water. Actually, I liked the cold water. Or was I fooling myself because I had gotten so used to it? I liked to smear the soap in my hands. Even though it did not foam, it was at least the symbol of hygiene and my face and hands were clean. Then I flung a handful of good cold water along my arms, over my chest and under and over the lower parts of my body. It felt so good. Finally, I rubbed my skin hard with a rough linen towel to get my blood circulating. It totally rejuvenated my system.

As I dressed in my room, I tracked back in time. Just last Wednesday I had been in Berlin to store my bicycle, and all other things I valued, in the basement of my mother-in-law's apartment. Today is Friday, April 20, 1945 — Hitler's birthday. Just 12 days ago I had turned 29. Here I was in Stahnsdorf, a suburb southwest of Berlin, and I was an instructor again. An instructor in charge of a squad of older men who had been drafted at the last minute. There was no demand for them in their positions as engineers, supervisors, or directors for war production. There was no more need of war production. Now it was time to defend our "Fatherland" however we could: with pitchforks or sticks in our hands, as Goebbels, the minister of Propaganda, had lately recommended.

Germany shrank day by day, pushed from both the east and the west. We knew the Americans were ready to cross the Elbe River. It could be only days, maybe hours, before they reached Berlin. Why are they not here yet?

With all the ups and downs and confusions of the war, for some reason I was called back as an instructor — first to Potsdam Radio Communications Barracks and now to Stahnsdorf. Here I was in charge of this group of "last hope." All through the war I had maintained my rank as a corporal in the Radio Communication Services.

The barracks in Stahnsdorf were filled to overflowing. The platoon I had been left in charge of was used for "permanent" field training and was moved out of the barracks into an earth hut half underground in the nearby forest. Since my room was in the barracks, I had to walk over to the forest to instruct and supervise my men. It was a good ten-minute walk. The men ate cold rations for the breakfast and evening meals in their forest quarters, but for lunch they went to the barracks dining hall. To make myself more flexible, I arranged for the *Gefreiter* (Lance Corporal) to walk the men over to the barracks and back.

The hut was romantically located at the edge of the forest where the trees were not too thick. The pathway from the barracks led over an open field. With a little cleverness one could know who was coming and going along the trail. The men always had someone on lookout duty so they could know in advance of any unannounced visitors — inspections, and so on. Some of the men's wives, living in nearby Berlin, came to visit their husbands. It was of special importance at those times to have a reliable man on lookout duty. In the dark of any night, one could see, hear, or just feel if someone was approaching.

I had a routine of whistling in the dark for at least the last couple hundred yards to the hut. And if I rode my bike, I rang its bell so they would know for sure it was just me. They knew I knew about the visits. It was a silent understanding between us.

After two years of radio communications training in Munich, I was released in 1937 as a corporal in the reserves. Now it was April 1945 and I was still a corporal. I had declined twice to be recommissioned as an officer cadet, so here I was, the same rank, playing the same game.

I had instructed my men to give a good impression when marching to the barracks so nobody would bother us. They were to be dressed properly, march in step, and smile, even if it hurt.

Most of the men were in their late 40s, and some were over 50. During the war years they held special positions in the war production. They were accustomed to giving orders. Now they had to learn to shout: "Yes, sir!"

Some of the men were not in the best physical condition for defending the *Vaterland*—to the last stone, the last tree, the last drop of blood. Still, they did well considering their age and physical condition. I had to smile when they came in through the gate of the barracks to the dining hall. Clean, they walked upright and in step. They had a gleam in their eyes and a song on their lips. Isn't that what you expect from a good soldier? If time allowed, I waited for them and for a brief moment looked into each man's eyes, and responded to him with a gleam in my own eyes. They knew there was an understanding heart inside my uniform with its few medals. I knew the game being played, and it had to be played to the bitter end. This end could not be too far away now.

The motto of the last few years had been, "Enjoy the war, the peace will be terrible—for a while! Do your best, no matter what comes." We did.

Feast During the marches between forest and camp, the men had seen rabbits running around. One evening at twilight I heard a bang—one shot, then silence. The next morning when I went to the men's hut, I could feel something in the air. They looked at each other as if to determine who would talk. Finally one of the men had the courage to report very officially, "We shot a hare last night."

It was a long time from hunting season, so I looked very serious about this "offense," and asked, "What did you do with it?"

"We cleaned and skinned it."

One of them then showed it to me.

"How in the world will you cook it?" I asked.

"We have a plan, but we need your help. One of our wives could prepare it in her kitchen at home, bring it out one evening, and we could all have a good meal. You will join us, won't you?"

I went back to the barracks and called the chosen man's wife, who could be reached only during the evening break at the factory where she worked. After several tries, I finally connected. She must have known about me. She understood right away when I told her the men had something for her to pick up, prepare, and bring back to them.

She was there the next afternoon to pick it up. The woman was clever. She brought a cardboard box along just in case. She did not know exactly what it might be, but she had a pretty good idea.

"Don't worry. I'll take care of it, and I'll be back tomorrow evening."

The men pitched in whatever they had.

"Here, take our butter ration, that will help."

"That will make a little bit of fat for the roasting."

We decided to save our bread rations, and looked forward to a real feast!

Bless that woman. She came the next evening. I was casually watching the way to the hut so that no interference by some "superior" could interrupt our well-planned feast. When she came, she brought along a neighbor. The hare was still in the roasting pan, wrapped in blankets and carried in a sack on her back. She needed help to get the hare right side up in the sack so nothing would spill out, and it would stay warm. The two of them decided to take their potato rations, cook them, and bring them along still in the peel and well wrapped to stay warm. The women carried the feast in a bag between them. When they came into the hut, the men's eyes grew big like little children, full of excitement. It was like Christmas in April. We all knew what was in the sack, but little did we know how good it would be. When the roasting pan was brought out of the blankets, the aroma permeated everything and called up pleasant memories of times gone by and home-cooked meals.

I was reminded of a cozy restaurant in Paris where I dined with a friend. The waiter served the food in covered plates. What a deliciously prepared meal we had that day in Paris. And now as the women lifted the cover of the pan, there were deep "Ahs" and "Ohs." There it was, the whole hare lying in the white gravy, well prepared with a spicy fragrance that filled the room. Normally there was an unpleasant odor. To our additional astonishment, she pulled the potatoes out of the bag. The husband had the honor of carving the roast. All of us took a portion of the meat and potatoes as well as that delicious gravy. No one touched the legs. It had not been talked over or arranged. It just happened.

In our excitement, we almost forgot to have someone on the lookout so no officer on duty would surprise us. All went well, however. Everyone enjoyed the meal and gave praises to our chefs. My eyes were moist as I conveyed my appreciation. That feast tied us all closer together!

"You were wonderful to do this for us," I said. "It was a delicious meal. Take the legs home for yourselves."

All the men echoed their appreciation to the two women. The main cook had to be on the night shift at the factory.

The Unexpected This Friday, April 20, 1945, was one of those sunny yet brisk spring days. We were standing in formation for the routine morning roll call. Something was in the air. We could detect real tension. The usually pleasant calm was unpleasant. Ignoring the obvious, I listened and enjoyed hearing the birds singing. It was springtime. The old soldier's song played in my mind: "When everything is green and blooming on this earth...."

I was daydreaming. The master sergeant snapped: "Morning, Company!"

"Morning, Master Sergeant," we answered.

The singing of the birds was overshadowed. The usual routine announcements passed through my ears. Suddenly someone kicked my butt.

The End at Last

"Corporal Schuetz, fall out!"

What had I done now? What had they found out? Did someone turn me in for something? I had gone to Berlin two days before to secure my bicycle and some of my belongings in my mother-in-law's basement. We were under strict orders not to leave the Stahnsdorf garrison. I had traveled with a special permit that was valid only from Potsdam to Berlin, but nobody had stopped me. I stepped forward, prepared for anything except to hear: "Corporal Schuetz, according to AVB, ... you are promoted to the rank of sergeant."

What an honor! Close to the end of the war, which would be over very soon anyway, I had been promoted.

Then it was announced: "All troops are placed on the highest alert. No one is to leave the barracks. No leave of any kind."

We went back to our quarters to prepare for the *Einsatz* (deployment). Our platoon had the privilege of walking out of the gate to the hut in the forest at anytime. I did not give orders for a song. I let them walk and talk. There was too much on their minds. For all of the questions they threw at me, I had no answers.

Here at the hut they congratulated me. The men thought my promotion was the best thing that could have happened. Maybe it made them proud to have a sergeant as their leader. It did not matter to me.

I gave them orders for the move. "Pack only the essential necessities that can be carried easily. There will be no transportation. We will have to walk and nobody knows how far or under what conditions."

I returned to the barracks to find out more details about our orders. No one could give me any decent answers. It was a madhouse! The only fact known for sure was that we had to get out of the barracks and get into position to defend Berlin, all that was left of the *Vaterland*. Details would come later.

Exodus I packed only what I knew I would need: wash gear, canteen, knife, fork, spoon, an extra pair of socks, and a couple of handkerchiefs. It all fit into a kind of sack I could hang from my belt. Finally I received a hand-drawn orientation paper and orders to leave with my men. After receiving our march ration for the day, we went in the ordered direction. Suddenly, there was a young lieutenant ordered to my troop. Since he was an officer I felt he should be in charge. But he left that to me.

He told me the next day: "You stay in charge, Schuetz, I feel out of place. The men and you are getting along very well."

I found out much later the men counted on me.

We marched for a couple of hours. Our defense was toward the west.

That night passed and nothing happened. With guards on duty, I saw to the comfort of my men in that strange atmosphere. It was very calm, like before a thunderstorm. In the far distance we heard the sound of artillery fire; *RUMS—RUMS*. I did not know exactly where we were. I had no answers to the many questions of my men other than, "Keep your eyes open; be on guard."

That morning a messenger came on bicycle to bring us new marching orders: straight south! I didn't like that, but maybe the Americans had swung around and were coming up from the south.

According to our orders, we came to a pretty good sized farm complex. Just outside the old, impressive wrought iron fence, an earthen bunker was prepared. It must have been built quite a while back, probably by the *Volksturm*, oldest of the old ones, or by the HJ — Hitler Jugend (Youth) — youngest of the young ones. We had a roof over our heads and lookouts along the road leading south. I made a schedule for guard duty to keep watch on the road to the south. I sent one man to watch the north in case anyone arrived with our food supply. This was Saturday, April 21. We had no rations. It was late afternoon, and the only thing we could get for nourishment was water from a hand pump in the middle of the farm courtyard.

The posts on both sides of the main farm entrance gate showed that the owner or manager must be an important man. Signs of the Party Group, the NSV (an NS social organization), and some other Nazi organizations were well displayed. I went to the farmhouse to try to get something to eat for my men.

"Do you have anything for my men to eat?" I asked the owner. "Even potatoes would be welcome."

"No, we don't even have enough for our own family," came the rude answer. Was the denial because I did not greet him with "Heil Hitler"?

The Party Is Over We spent the night in our underground quarters. It was not too cold. With the coming of morning we wondered what the day would bring. We had plenty of water from the pump for a good morning wash and plenty to drink. By noon, I went to the owner again to get something for the men. I was walking across the farmyard toward the house when he came out. I thought he must be expecting me. I saluted him.

"Our supplies have not yet reached us and we would appreciate anything you might be able to spare for us to eat."

Without responding to my request, he walked toward the gateposts. To my utter surprise he pulled down the Nazi signs he once had so proudly displayed so that anyone passing by would know what an important party leader he was. He had only a few words for me, and with fear in his eyes, he said: "The Russians are coming!"

I looked at the four holes left for every sign he had pulled off. Like bloody tears, the red brick dust out of those holes trickled down the covered-over white stucco. I mumbled to myself, "This is all that is left of the thousand-year Reich. This is the end."

I kicked at a clod of dirt and headed back to the men. In the same moment came the reality that I was responsible for their well-being. We had known each other for only a few weeks. Yet every one was a human being, a person, precious to his family — a father, husband, son. I felt they were a part of me. I could not demand the defense of the *Vaterland* to the last square meter. I knew what I had to do. I went straight to the bunker. The men were waiting for me to come with good news of some kind of food supply. I made sure all the men were there, then I announced short, direct, and to the point:

"Lieutenant, men, I could not get a bite of food out of the SOB. He just tore down the signs at his gateposts and told me, 'The Russians are coming!' If anyone sees tanks coming up the road, do not shoot the bazooka. If you do and miss, or even hit a tank, they will throw a grenade into our bunker and we will be blown to bits. I have been in battles with tanks in the Caucasus. They come in bunches, one protecting the other.

"Lieutenant, you are officially the commander in charge. I recommend we set the men free. Some might want to try to get through to Berlin. Those who don't want to risk it can stay and see what comes."

The lieutenant replied, "I think Schuetz is right. Make up your minds and do what you think is best." Turning to me: "Schuetz, have you decided?"

"Yes, Lieutenant. If all want to go, then I will go with them. If anyone decides to stay, I will stay."

We did not know how close the Russians were. There were no long emotional farewells. Within minutes most of the men were gone, including the lieutenant. There were eight of us left. Fortunately, we did not know what would come. We just waited. Waited for what? Yes, waited for it all to be over. My calmness astonished me. I had a deep peace inside. I was waiting for the end of what had started five and a half years before. Memories flashed back: talks with my father. He was killed just three months ago by bombs in Düsseldorf.

That very night I was on duty as UvD in the Potsdam Radio Communication barracks. A phone call came through on the outside line.

"UvD3. Company, Corporal Schuetz speaking," I said.

"This is the Air Force Switchboard West. I cannot give you the location. We have been trying for days to get through to you. Are you Corporal Hansarmin Schuetz?"

"Yes, I am."

"Your father was killed on January 23 by bombs during the day at the Franklin School in Düsseldorf. Try to get leave to take care of his belongings. See Mr. and Mrs. ——— where your father lived during his last days. *Click — Click...*"

We were interrupted. I did not get to say thank you to that communications helper for her efforts to reach me. I just happened to be on duty that night and answered that phone call. As I stepped out of the office into the darkened hallway, a smile came to my face: "Father, you are spared, you don't have to go through this horror and see the end of this war!"

Some of the talks we had together came back to me. Whenever we had a chance to visit during the war, he often said: "Hansarmin, don't make it so hard on yourself. You are a soldier and you have to carry out orders, whatever they are. You fight these Nazis in every part that is in you."

My answer came again and again: "Father, this is the price we have to pay. We have to lose this war to get rid of Hitler and the Nazi Party — the Nazi Gang. It is the only way. If Hitler wins the war, we will always be soldiers in order to keep the captured territories occupied. It will be a continuous war even with the peace."

I got that leave. I traveled to Düsseldorf for my father's funeral. On the way back I arranged to stop over in Erfurt to visit my wife, Annemarie, and son Hans in Stotternheim and my mother in Saalfeld. I wanted to bring my mother the news about father's death myself.

An End and a Beginning

"Davai, Uri!" I had to grasp reality. Was I prepared for this kind of end after five and a half years of war?

I gave orders to take the bazooka out of the slot in the bunker so no one would get trigger-happy and shoot it off. I listened to the rolling tanks. Some stopped close to our bunker. We could hear the motor of one idling next to the entrance. We remained silent, nobody said a word. I could feel all eyes directed toward me. They seemed to be asking: What will he do? What next? The door was suddenly kicked open. A Russian tank commander wearing a leather jacket came toward me, his pistol cocked and ready to shoot. I had the honor of being the first to be captured. The first words he spoke were "*Davai, uri,*" and with that he took my watch. Then he asked for my pistol. He collected the *uris* (watches) from everyone and directed us out of our hole in the ground.

Not far behind the gate in the farmyard was a little octagonal building. It appeared to be only a roof coming out of the ground. We had never paid much attention to it. It had small windows close to the ground and a door. One of the Russian soldiers kicked the door open. It led to a small basement room. He yelled to us to come, "*Davai, davai,*" and pointed through the doorway down the stairs. That was to be our jail until they decided what to do with us on a more permanent basis. We crawled down the stairs. We were happy everything had culminated quickly and no harm had been done to any of us. The room was dark. It was about eight feet in diameter, and as our eyes adjusted we discovered shelves along the outside walls. There was just enough space for eight guys to sit around in a circle. We saw canned food in glass jars stored all around us. The room we were locked in seemed to be the pantry for the farmhouse. Before the men could express their joyful surprise, I put my fingers to my lips and pointed up the stairs to the closed door. It was better if those above did not know what we had found down here. The men could not see well enough to tell what they were grabbing off the shelves, but it was food!

Not Given but Taken We hadn't had a decent meal in over two days. The poor Nazi farmer had said he had nothing to spare for us. Now we had it all for ourselves. As we opened one jar after the other, we ate with our fingers and passed the containers around. Jar after jar made the rounds, and the empty ones were set in the middle of the circle. All this activity was done in complete silence. We were excited about this great feast! I had to dampen their spirits from time to time by putting my finger to my lips. The only interruption was the not-too-loud *pop* as a new jar was opened. It was a surprise dinner because we didn't know what was in each jar until it was open, we had sampled it, and passed it on. We tasted chicken, vegetables, green beans, peaches, beef, pears (sweet, soft, and juicy). I had always loved pears, and could never stop after eating just one. There were green peas, too, which were a little difficult to get out with our fingers. Someone was smart enough to dump the water out of that jar and pour the peas straight into his mouth.

Then came some pork (good and fat like in the old days). Our fingers were soon sweet and greasy. We really knew what it meant to be "finger-lickin' good." We ate and ate, not knowing when we would taste food again.

It was a blessing when a Russian soldier opened the door and called us out, "*Davai, davai,*" waving his hand for us to come up. I barely had a chance to point, indicating nobody was to take anything with them. As we went up the narrow stairs one by one, we wiped our greasy mouths on the sleeves of our uniforms. The guards checked us for guns and watches. It was a wonder we did not burp in their faces. If we had been down there another fifteen or twenty minutes, we would all have been sick. It was good timing.

The Russians repeated one word often, "*Davai, davai,*" pointing to the road leading south. As we walked down the road, we counted forty-two tanks lined up. They seemed to be on a rest stop and the crews were glad to get out of the crowded tanks. The basic words repeated so often were:

"*Fritz kaputt.*" "*Nix Hitler.*" "*Hitler Kaputt.*" "*Davai, davai*" encouraged us to keep moving. "*Voyna* (war) *kaputt.*" "*Damoi, damoi.*" "*Skoro damoi.*"

We had no idea of the meaning of some of the words. Some Russians spit at us. There were harsh words that must have been curses. We kept moving. As we entered a forest, we came to an area I remembered from my childhood. My family had lived in a suburban area south of Berlin. I had spent most of my school years there. We had pedaled our bicycles over the countryside visiting schoolmates. I must have mentioned to the men that I knew this area. They realized it and kept close to me. When I stopped to take a leak on a tree, they pretended to be doing the same. My men were watching me more carefully than the Russians. Along the way we met other Russian soldiers. They pointed in the southern direction: "*Davai, komrad, davai.*"

We kept going. Slowly we started talking more to each other to keep up our spirits. After our initial shock, we began to realize the war was over and we would be home before long.

An End and a Beginning

We heard artillery fire in a southeasterly direction. Sometimes it was quite intense, then again there were long pauses in between. We kept going.

"*Davai, davai,*" shouted the Russians crossing our path.

Our thoughts went to those soldiers who had left for Berlin. Had they made it through without enemy contact as well as avoiding German Military Police? We had heard stories that deserters were shot on the spot. We came to Kleinbeeren where we joined other captured German soldiers. Everyone was in a good mood and glad the war was over at last. As we entered the village we were stopped, and for the first time someone took charge of us. We did not see any civilians in this village. Either they had fled before the Russians came, or they were ordered to stay inside.

The Russians began to decide our fate. They talked back and forth. We did not understand the words but could tell by the tone of their conversation there was some disagreement. One gesture indicated they should shoot all of us. They argued a bit more, then came to an agreement: "*Davai, komrad, komm, davai.*"

We got up from the sitting position.

Close Call One of the soldiers had found a safe place to keep us overnight — the cellar of a farmhouse that had only one entrance from the outside. The trap door was opened.

"*Davai, davai.*"

Down we went into the dark. Our numbers had grown to twenty German soldiers, or rather, prisoners of war. We entered a clean, dry basement room. The farmer used it to store his grain. It was quite dark, but a ray of light filtered in and we were able to orient ourselves. We crawled on top of the grain sacks and made a bed for the night. This night's quarters was to be one of the best we would experience for a long time to come. Having gorged ourselves just a few hours ago, my little group was not hungry, but some of the newcomers had not eaten for days. They helped themselves to the grain kernels. I later learned how nourishing whole grain kernels are. If you grind them really fine with your teeth, they become almost like flour in your mouth. Nourishing, yes, but they make you thirsty, and there was no water in that cellar. We were all too tired to talk that night. Everyone slept well on those grain-filled sacks.

Daylight was sneaking in through the cracks of the door. We heard voices and someone shouted: "*Davai, davai, komrad.*"

It sounded like a wake-up signal. The first Russian, with his MP, came down the stairs with his gun pointed toward us. He was ready to mow us down. A second one followed right behind him. Then a ranking Russian entered who must have been in charge. He said something that we could not understand exactly.

We understood enough to know he was about to check us out for guns, ammunition, watches, whatever he might find that would be of value. When it came my turn I was ready to step forward knowing I had nothing with me anymore. I wore my overcoat and put my hands in the pockets to hold it open for the check. I felt something in my left pocket. I knew immediately what it was. But how had it gotten there? Evidently someone standing next to me knew we would be thoroughly checked and slipped it into my overcoat pocket. In all the moving around and touching each other, I had not noticed. Here I was stuck with an egg-shaped hand grenade! I made a sudden reverse movement — one step back — and dropped the hand grenade into an open grain sack. I checked myself again to be sure I did not carry any "gifts" from someone else.

Finally I stepped forward, was checked, and with an almost friendly "*Davai*" went up the stairs into the daylight. The guards outside were hospitable. They let us use the hand pump to wet our faces, drink, and fill up with water. The ones who had eaten the grain kernels the night before especially needed that drink. As other German prisoners of war joined us, guards were watching us. We got into formation and marched down the village street, continuing south. One thing puzzled us: There was still the sound of artillery in the distance.

A Little White Bag We noticed Russian soldiers, not armed, walking in our same direction. They were in a good mood, talking to each other and laughing. There was no hostility toward us.

I was walking in the middle of the row of five. I knew instinctively to act sensibly and keep everything low key. This had worked well. There was still a silver band around the collar of my uniform indicating rank.

Out of nowhere a Russian stepped right into our formation. He came straight toward me. He had a face that scared me: black bushy hair, black fiery eyes, and skin full of scars. He was the type who asked no questions, just did what he had to do or wanted to do. He looked straight into my eyes and said something in Russian. It was not *Davai*. I did not understand much except the word *sergeant*. He handed me a clean little white cotton bag and stepped out of our column. Before I realized what he was doing, he was gone. I looked down at the little white bag. It was full of bread cut into pieces. I took slice after slice from the bag and broke each in half, passing them to the men. Some thanked me, to which I responded, "Do not thank me, thank that wild-looking Russian sergeant."

I thanked that Russian sergeant many times in my thoughts. That little white bag was precious to me. It was my first "possession" since our capture.

As we walked along, our group grew larger. Things became more organized. We had an escort with soldiers on each side and two at the end. There would be no more thoughts of escape. To impress us, the Russians shot once in a while into the air. They laughed at us when we showed no reaction. We were not impressed.

Walk, walk.

"*Davai*" from the front and "*Davai*" from the rear.

We had to keep moving. As we came more into Russian-occupied territory we saw many soldiers and camps, open fires, some army kitchen setups. There

An End and a Beginning

The brew turned into a good solid stew.

was confusion. It did not appear well organized, but it must have served its purpose.

Seek and Ye Shall Find We had learned to guess the time of day by the position of the sun. It must have been late afternoon when the guards stopped us on the outskirts of a little village. They gestured that they would be back in a minute, and left us completely on our own. We were beside a half-burned-out farmhouse. Our first thought was to find something to eat. We mingled freely among other Russian soldiers. Nobody bothered us. We scouted around, exploring the situation. One of our men found the head of a cow. We assumed it was discarded from a Russian field kitchen. To cook it we needed a pot, water, firewood, and matches. All the men in my group went in different directions and came back with something. One brought a pot. In the burned-out house we found enough firewood, and with discarded bricks we built a makeshift stove. One man skinned the head with his pocketknife. We stopped a Russian soldier walking by and asked for matches to start the fire. He thought we wanted cigarettes, but we showed him our stove with the cow head ready to be cooked. He laughed and taught us a new word; "*Khorosho*" (good). He gave us matches and three cigarettes. We started cooking the cow head — snout, teeth, brains, and all. We smoked the cigarettes one at a time, passing each around from man to man so everyone had the same amount of puffs.

All of a sudden we realized one of our men was missing. He was the slow-moving type, fairly tall, with a long face and very bushy eyebrows that grew together — kind of the way I would have looked if I had let my eyebrows grow together. I had started to pull out the eyebrows that grew over my nose when I was about fourteen years old. With him, they seemed to belong there. We finally saw him coming. He was moving slowly. His eyes were constantly moving, observing everything around him. We told him how sorry we were that he missed the cigarettes. He didn't say a word. He began to unload his pockets and out came potatoes and more potatoes. There must have been ten pounds or more.

"I thought we could use something besides that cow head," he said.

I asked, "Where did you find them?"

I never got an answer. Maybe he was afraid to get anybody else involved.

We cleaned the potatoes with water and our fingernails and dumped them into our pot with the cow head. We let the whole mess cook for an hour or so. What is an hour more or less if you have nothing else to do? The brew turned into a good solid stew, salt-free, with what little meat the cow head provided. We ate from aluminum canteens, pieces of wood, whatever we could find to serve as a plate. It was a real stew and not just soup. It tasted great!

Some Russians passing by who were a little intoxicated said: "*Damoi, skoro damoi*!"

We found out that it means, "*Nach hause, bald nach hause*" ("Home, soon home!").

We didn't know if they meant us, too. They were gone. We were gone. We could not ask them anymore questions.

Interrogation In the middle of the night a Russian soldier came for me with his rifle, ready to pull the trigger.

"*Davai, komrad.*"

He pointed to indicate I should go with him. I came out of a deep sleep after that nourishing meal. It took me a moment to orient myself. Yes, I was a prisoner of war. I finally understood I was to go with him. The thought ran around in my mind: Had someone found out about those potatoes? I got up half awake and was escorted by the young Russian soldier. He was a clean-cut lad, not angry or hostile, almost polite. We entered a house with a guard at the door. There was light only from candles and oil lamps. Smoke hung down from the low ceiling in the small room. We advanced through a hallway to another room. My escort exchanged some words with a man in the doorway. He seemed to be glad to see me. In the dim light I could see he wore a uniform indicating a rank insignia. He asked me in perfect German where I had come from and if I had seen Hitler. He knew I was from a radio communications unit. I wondered how he could know. The only sign that revealed our army unit was the very small yellow cord along the edge of our caps. I wondered if he had his men scouting for members of those special army units. I could sense he respected me. I told him I had come from Berlin. Yes, I had seen Hitler many years ago in Munich where

An End and a Beginning

I studied photography. It was the day Hitler opened the construction site for a future subway system. It must have been in the fall of 1937 or spring of 1938. He smiled. He did not want to know my past. He wanted to know if I had seen Hitler lately. He offered me a cigarette and came around close and asked me directly:

"Do you know where Hitler is? Did you have radio contact with the station close to him?"

Finally I understood and knew I had an advantage. This poor Russian officer was desperate to know where Hitler was. I started to question him.

"My men and I want to know where we are?"

He smiled and said, "I cannot tell you."

I questioned again. "Why not?"

He smiled again and said, "It is better for a prisoner of war not to know where he is."

To know would make it easier to escape. Now it was his turn to question me.

"Do you have any idea where Hitler could be? Is he still alive?"

He kept coming back to the same question in the hope that I might give him some kind of a hint. Finally he gave up. I hit him with a question:

"How do you speak German so well?"

I saw a flicker in his eyes like I had hit a soft spot. I could tell he was upset by my curiosity. He said, "I studied it."

He called the guard. I had one last question. "What time is it?"

He pointed to his watch, which was bigger than a silver dollar. It showed 4:00 A.M. He added, "This is Moscow time."

He must have known Germany was two hours behind, and for us it would be about two o'clock in the morning. I thanked him for the cigarette and departed. We were two men coming from different cultures and situations but meeting almost on a human basis. We both made a gesture almost like a handshake. We bade each other goodnight. On the way back to my quarters the guard tried to tell me the commandant was "*khorosho*." There was that new word again. I was learning Russian slowly, and my intuition told me it would be the best thing to do.

My men had not slept since I was taken away. They felt lost without me. Their voices expressed how they felt more than words. They were glad and exclaimed: "Hansarmin is back."

There was not much sleep that night. They wanted to know all of the details of what had happened to me. One of them said: "Did you ask him when we could go home?"

What a silly question. The Russian wouldn't know anyway. He wasn't Stalin. It puzzled me why the Russian officer had picked me to question. Who was he that he spoke German so well? He was, I decided, just a human being like me. With that I went to sleep.

Marching to a Different Drummer

A Long Walk The next morning we had no time to heat our leftover cow head and potato stew. Our new guards made so much commotion getting us together that it appeared they were trying to impress someone special. We grabbed a handful of the cold, stiff stew and stuffed it into our mouths. A second handful we ate more slowly as we started walking. It was to be our last meal for a long time. As we assembled, more and more German prisoners came from everywhere into our formation. We must have been a hundred now. More joined us as we walked. The sound of artillery fire came closer. Our Russian guards were nervous and kept us moving. They were not so friendly and were more experienced in transporting prisoners. We were required to walk in strict formation and at a fast pace. Those too weak to keep up were dragged along by others. My men were in good shape compared to others.

One older fellow, pale and undernourished, could not make it. We encouraged him, lifted him, carried him; he was so light. He begged us leave him. He pleaded: "Please let me go. I cannot keep up anymore." He walked slowly. The marching men behind us passed him by. When we stopped for the night, he was not with us.

Our guards locked us up in an empty barn. They had a tough job. During the day they marched with us, carrying their rifles. At night they had to stand guard duty so none of us would escape. We were too tired to think about escaping. Our ration was only two buckets of water. How good a swallow of water tasted! And how good to lie down on the bare dirt of the barn floor and rest.

There was enough room for me to stretch out. It was almost comfortable, but something stuck in my back. I figured it was two little rocks. I scraped them out in the pitch dark. My fingernail cut into one of them. What a surprise — two potatoes about the size of an egg. Something to eat! There were only strangers around me. How could I eat a raw potato without making any noise biting and chewing? I scraped the potato on my lower teeth very slowly with hardly a sound. The potato shavings dissolved in my mouth. It was a slow process, but the more

I scraped, the slower I "ate," the better it tasted. I was having a real meal after a long day of walking.

The next morning our guards had something for us to eat. It was warm and thick. Those who did not have a container had to get their portion in their hands or be passed by. We learned that they called it "*kasha*."

We got used to the long days of walking. Mornings or evenings there was something to eat. Not much, but enough to survive. The occasional slice of bread was a delight. As the days went by, the artillery fire got even closer. It was to the east of us. The Russians were tense. We were not allowed to step out of the marching order. If we did, they would shoot into the air. Those marching in the front section wondered if someone marching behind had been shot.

Most of the time we walked along the *autobahn* (highway). Walking on concrete was hard on our feet. By evening we were so tired we were glad just to lie down, physically exhausted and mentally unable to think realistically. We were glad to get a bite to eat and hopefully a decent night's rest. In our thoughts and dreams we wanted to escape, but we did not have the strength. We learned to take things moment by moment and prayed only for enough strength to make it through another day.

There was always someone in worse shape. We encouraged the weaker ones and watched them gain strength as one does when someone else cares. Without realizing it, we carried one another's burdens. We were all together in the same misery.

Wasted Effort It was a relief when we left the *autobahn* and walked on a secondary road that led through villages. The change was welcome. We saw houses, people, exchanged a word here and there, and got to see what condition the villages were in. We speculated about what they had gone through.

The residents of one village must have been expecting us. All along the road, almost in front of every house, was either a basket or box with sandwiches neatly packed. We just had to reach out and grab one. There was water and milk in pots and pans along the way. What a pleasant surprise!

However, the guards gave strict orders not to touch anything. They shot into the pots and cans and into the sandwich piles. The milk and water soaked into the ground and the sandwiches burst into the air and fell into the dirt. We did not dare touch anything. We could see women who had prepared all this food with love and sacrifice standing behind the windows and in doorways. The expressions on their faces mirrored us to be a bunch of dirty, tired, hungry, and thirsty German prisoners who were dragging along the way.

Where were the *landser*, the well-dressed German soldiers, clean-cut, well-fed, marching in step, singing a rousing song with a spark in their eyes? What had happened? We were the same men. But the circumstances now were far different. The past was gone, and a kind of hopelessness prevailed.

Seeing that water, milk, and sandwiches going to waste startled us to understand our true condition. We were in great need, and longed to just reach out and help ourselves to these gifts of food. We recognized the love and compassion of those German women in that little village. For their efforts they received bullet holes in their water pots and milk cans.

What happened was a real shock. For a long time nobody said anything. Slowly remarks began to come, and did they keep us going for the rest of the day!

Another night, another day, walking, walking, walking. The only good thing was the blacktop roads. We came through some villages but never had another welcome like this one. Word must have spread.

Service: Hospital Style As we entered one of the villages, people in white shirts behind the windows stared out at us. The entire village had been made into a field hospital. Every home owner had given up rooms for sick and wounded Russian soldiers. I remembered my brother Waldemar, who was five years older than me, a battalion physician in the front lines who was southeast of Charkov (Kharkov) in the winter of 1941–42. A war reporter sent us pictures of him at his first aid station taking care of wounded and frostbitten German soldiers as well as civilians and children.

He was supposed to come home for his first leave from the battlefield in January. But someone else took his place and he had to wait until this person returned. Waldemar grew a beard out of protest. On February 15, 1942, Russian tanks broke through the lines and came into this village. Waldemar was hit by a tank grenade, or something else bigger than a rifle. It struck him under his left shoulder and tore open his lungs. His orderly wrote us later about how he had encouraged him: "Doctor, everything will be alright."

But Waldemar knew how critically he was wounded. He had wanted to become a specialist in lung diseases. They laid him in a wooden wardrobe filled with straw to protect him against the frost, and transported him on a sled to the next field hospital where he died the next morning.

Turning a village into a field hospital was nothing unusual. I thought: Waldemar, you did the same thing to provide a bed and shelter for your men; to bring them out of the cold. You expressed many times in your letters that you did not have enough medication or sufficient warm clothes for the men standing guard duty outside. Men with first- and second-degree frostbite had to be sent out on guard duty again because there was not enough manpower to replace them.

We came to a stop right in the middle of the village. Wounded Russian soldiers rushed out of the houses, some on crutches. We were presented to them like war trophies. Some lifted up their crutches as though to hit us, and cursed us in a language we did not understand. The Russians around us laughed. They understood what they were saying. We could feel the hatred. But who could blame them? They had lost limbs, maybe a friend or brother. We stood there, helpless and spit on. In disgrace. How tired physically and mentally we were!

Some of my fellow prisoners of war were almost children, only 15 or 16 years of age. They were drafted at the very end of the war to defend the *Vaterland*. They begged for something to eat.

"Give us a piece of bread."

Those young ones suffered more than the older men. Their whole world was gone; a world they had grown up in. Their hopes were destroyed. They were taught to believe in the Führer and the Third Reich, and it had all vanished into emptiness. Everything they believed in had been a lie. There they were, begging for something to eat. A Russian came with a bedpan full of soup, and those kids laid flat on their bellies and slurped the soup out of the bedpan.

Did those Russians do it out of compassion or did they set a dirty bedpan filled with nourishing soup down before the Germans to see what they would do? I had to turn away. I didn't want to know the answer to that question.

It was a relief when we could march again, and leave insult and laughter behind. It was more comfortable to keep going step by step and to be free with our thoughts.

My mind traveled back to the day I took my bicycle to my mother-in-law's house to store it until my return; then to my last visit with my wife Annemarie and son Hans, when he was just a little over three years old. They are in Thuringia now with the Americans. Annemie. I called her Annemie. I talk a lot with you in my thoughts.

I wonder if I did the right thing when I was in Düsseldorf at my father's funeral in late January? One could hear the artillery in the distance day and night. I thought of hiding in Düsseldorf. Father had a lot of friends in the city, and I could have stayed with them until the Americans came. I could have worn father's leftover suits, a little old fashioned, but they would have served the purpose. I could have lived on his rations for a while before it had to be reported he had been killed. I thought about you, Annemie and Hans. What would they have done to you if they had found out, and to my mother? For that reason I returned to active duty. Now I am here, Annemie, and I am glad you can't see me. I send you my thoughts with all of my strength, that you may have peace and receive the message that I am still alive.

I began gradually to accept my fate and to realize we were in God's hands, and He would take care of us. This thought became more meaningful to me, Annemie, than the words we spoke when we said good-bye:

"*Bleib Gott befohlen.*" (Know that you are in God's plan.)

It would have been better to have stayed on the *autobahn*, even though the concrete was hard on our feet, than to travel these back roads through the villages and suffer humiliation. We had no thought of escaping anymore. We were thankful only to make it through each day and not be left behind, dead.

It must have been the first week of May, since we had excellent weather throughout our trip. The days were sunny but not too warm, and the nights were not too cool. Most of us still wore our army overcoats and covered up at night when we stretched out on the dirt floor. Some rolled them up to make a pillow.

End of the Trail! Or...? We finally reached Sagan (Zagan), about 150 miles southeast of Berlin, and walked right into a camp on the outskirts of the city that had been occupied by former American or Russian prisoners of war. During the march, our German group had grown by now to several hundred. The camp was almost like paradise! Every man got a bunk and three meals a day, mostly hot soup with not too much substance, but hot. There was running water in one of the barracks, and we could wash every morning and evening if we wanted to. There were no towels, but we dried ourselves in the sun — a pleasant experience.

Trees and bushes came forth with green leaves. There was a fragrance in the air, which we had not noticed during our march. We were finally at our destination. A place to rest — it felt so good. In the middle of the camp there was a slight incline and a beautiful view of the surrounding area.

I did not mind staying in that camp and working in the city or for a farmer in the neighborhood. Whatever they assigned was okay. As soon as the war was over, we would go home. Berlin was not too far away. We could go back the way we came, catching a ride with a farmer driving home from his work in the fields, be invited to a meal, stay overnight, and receive a packed lunch to carry us over the days to come. We would keep going, going home.

Hey, wake up — stop dreaming, Hansarmin — you have just arrived in a prisoner of war camp. That was the true reality!

It Is Finished!

Tears They assembled us on that hillside. A Russian officer stood at the very top of the hill and read an official announcement in Russian. An interpreter translated for us: Hitler was dead. The German Army had surrendered, von Doenitz had signed the paper for the German government. The war was officially over. A roar of approval came from the German soldiers. The end of the war. Could it be true? Would we be going home now?

I thought back to the day when I had first realized the end was in sight. It was the 6th of June, 1944. I was riding in an open vehicle toward a partisan area close to Lemberg (now Lvov) in what was then Poland, but occupied by the German Army. Among us was a fairly young lieutenant with the *Ritterkreuz*. As our truck came to a stop to let other traffic go by, a soldier from below called up to us:

"The Americans have invaded Normandy!"

Without thinking, I said a little too jubilantly, more to myself than to anybody, but loud enough to be heard: "This is the beginning of the end!"

The lieutenant turned toward me like a streak of lightning and with an angry voice shouted: "Schuetz, how can you say something like that, or even have a thought in that direction?"

He was furious. I stood at attention, saluted, and replied:

"Yes sir, Lieutenant."

I continued to dwell on the fact that this was the truth whether they wanted to see it or not. It was the price we had to pay to get rid of Hitler and the Nazis.

On that hillside in that Russian prison camp on a beautiful, sunny spring day came the announcement:

"It is finished."

As I slowly went down the hill, tears came to my eyes. I was not ashamed. It was too emotional and overwhelming. I let go. A guy laid his arm around my shoulder trying to comfort me and said, "Don't take it so seriously, we can start anew again."

My tears were tears of joy, not of sorrow. I don't think he understood, and left feeling sorry for me.

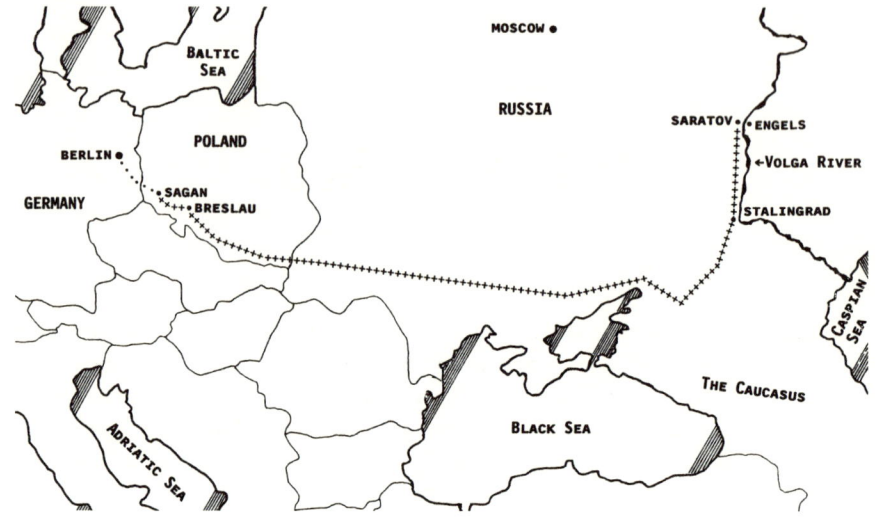

Route of the German prisoners across Russia to the camps.

The Sagan prison camp looked even better after receiving this wonderful news. It was a pleasant place with full room and board, a bunk to lie down on at night, three meals a day, and cold, running water. We could survive here until they sent us home. Some of the prisoners had steady jobs and went out to work every morning, but most hung around the camp. All kinds of news circulated through the camp, but nothing could be confirmed. Someone always heard the latest and came back to report.

"The German people killed Hitler."

"The Russians and Americans killed Hitler."

"Hitler killed himself."

"All prisoners of war will be going home tomorrow."

"All prisoners of war will be going home in two months."

Each man sorted out what he wanted to hear. It was amusing. The rumors between men blossomed as little things were added or left out. It was best not to listen at all.

Lingering around the camp we noticed a formation gathering and went up close to find out what was going on. We were immediately put into a line. German prisoners of war were in charge. They were well-fed, tough guys, with authority from a higher command.

The order was for a thousand men for a transport. They worked in teams of three and four grabbing men and commanding them to move to the assembly place. It was impossible to escape. I looked around and counted five of our men who had been caught. They yelled at us to walk in rows of five. Not far down the line we passed a Russian officer who did the actual counting. How many rows of five equal a thousand? As we continued to move along, Russian soldiers guarded our march out the gate — to where? Were we going home today?

Rolling via Railroad How lucky, no more walking; we were to go by train. A long row of boxcars waited for us. But there was no locomotive on the train. Grouped into seven rows of five, with a "*Davai, davai,*" thirty-five men crawled into a boxcar. The door shut tight with a click as it was locked from the outside. Five of our original group were together in the fifth or sixth railroad car. We sat against the outside wall. Slowly we got used to the darkness and discovered that the vent slots high up in the wall were shut, nailed form the outside. Those cattle cars must have been used many times for transporting herds of human beings.

Somebody exclaimed: "Were these same boxcars used to transport people from concentration camps or Russian prisoners of war, and now us?"

I contemplated: If these walls could talk, what grief, tears, and agony they would relate. It's best that they remain silent.

It was enough that we did not know where these boxcars would carry us, what the future held, and where we would end up; so many questions, and no answers.

Boxed In The five of us stuck together. The experiences we had endured over the past three weeks had bound us tightly together. Our relationships had turned into solid friendships. We would share and suffer together.

Night came. We heard the noise of switching rail cars, trains running by. The guards walked along the train and we heard them shuffling on the rocks along the track. Their walks became less frequent. Once in a while someone opened a boxcar door, and there was a little commotion, sometimes close, sometimes far away.

We wondered if they would check us in every car, but they never came near. We were locked in a railroad car sitting on the tracks, but not moving. I fell asleep.

The light of day brought life into our car. The sun rose in the east and sent one little ray of light through a hole that showed up on the opposite wall as a tiny light spot. Someone held his hand over the spot and the light showed up in his palm. This way we located the hole, which was so small that we would have never found it if it had not been for this ray of light. One of the men who still had his pocketknife began to enlarge the opening. It was fairly quiet in the rail yard. We heard some switching activity far away. Amazing the noise the little knife blade made on the dried-up wood plank! Maybe we were just oversensitive. A guy held his ear to the outside wall and said, "Psst," as guards approached each side of the train. The guard on the east side concerned us most. We heard him coming and going with an even step, walking on the rocks beside the tracks. We gave the carver a sign to stop, held our breath and listened to our heartbeats. We wanted to make the hole just big enough to catch the name of a passing railroad station so we would at least know the direction of our travels. By now the hole was about the size of a pea, and even with our work one could not fit a little finger in it yet.

We heard some commotion outside the train. It came closer. Our door opened and one man had to get out. In the moment the door opened, a guy in the corner felt a draft from the floor. We discovered a hole in the floor about the size of a hand. That hole must have been used for a toilet by the previous occupants. We could now relieve ourselves decently, but it took some doing to hit the hole, especially in the dark.

There was more commotion outside and orders were given in Russian. "*Davai, davai.*" The sliding door on the car next to ours opened. There was talk, and *slam*. It was locked again. The steps advanced to our car; our door slid open. The man we had sent for water was trying to lift a bucket to the floor of the boxcar. Two of our men jumped up to help him and managed to get it in. The bucket was full of warm water. It was our breakfast.

Some of the men still had their canteens, a spoon, or an aluminum cup. Using these we divided the water fairly among us. It amounted to about one cup per man. A small amount of water was left and since nobody was in command, to avoid a fight, I took charge.

"Let's not fight over the bit of water. It would be good to dump it around our latrine to dilute the smell," I suggested. "We don't know how long we will be in this car and the smell is quite penetrating."

Everyone seemed to agree. But after we did the job, I wondered if it was such a good idea after all. That bit of warm water around the hole made the odor stronger than before, but soon we did not notice it anymore. Maybe we got used to it. To pass the time some of the men tried to walk around. Others joined in. As more and more men got up off the floor and joined in the walk, we had room enough to walk in a tight circle. That was our only exercise, and it became routine for us.

As the day dragged on, railroad traffic increased, switchers were running by, and we heard a whistle sound here and there. It was interesting to listen and wonder what was really going on outside. Later on the guards brought us some bread. Thirty-five slices — one slice per man. I broke my slice into bite-size pieces and chewed each bite very slowly.

I thought about Tante Else, a friend from my mother's youth, who invited us all for Sunday dinner once in a while. She had two sons too, but her boys were a little older than Waldemar and I. It was the custom in Germany to serve soup at the start of dinner. Tante Else reminded her sons to chew the soup even if there was nothing much to chew. Maybe there was something to the idea of letting the food in your mouth saturate with saliva, making it more nourishing. That's what I did with my bread, and how I enjoyed it! I spent much more time eating my slice of bread than the others, but there was nothing else to do anyway; nothing to do and no place to go.

It Is Finished! 29

An Expensive Hole I asked the fellow with the knife to let me use it for a while. As I carved on the hole, the cars suddenly jerked and couplings cracked. They hooked up a locomotive on the north end of the train. We heard the guards running along the track to get into their convoy car. Soon we started to move.

The task of increasing the size of the hole became more important if we were to get a glimpse of the outside world. The larger blade now fit into the hole and carved much better. Looking halfway down, I could see the tracks next to us. *Click—click.* We crossed a switch, and I saw what I assumed was a Polish switchman waiting to let our train pass by so he could turn the switch by hand. When he looked up, I got a glimpse of his face. He must have seen the knife blade halfway through the hole, for he shouted something to somebody. I continued carving. The original little hole was now good sized and we could see out fairly well. Suddenly the train came to a stop and the locomotive was taken off. We heard the Russian guards coming alongside the train. They stopped at our car and banged against the wall, signaling that we should help from the inside to open the sliding door. The guards unlocked the door and opened it far enough so that we could get a hold from the inside and push it all the way open. The barrels of two rifles faced us, held by two soldiers still standing on the ground. Three soldiers jumped into our car. Two of them were holding cocked rifles. The third seemed to be in charge and demanded something in Russian. One of our men understood enough to translate:

"Where is the knife and who bore a hole in the side of the boxcar?"

The Russians acted like we had blown the boxcar apart and were ready to escape. The same question came again:

"Where is the knife and who bore a hole in the side of the boxcar?"

We were all standing around the three Russians in the middle.

"If the guilty one will not come forward, you will all be shot."

They made gestures with the rifles as if to shoot everyone. No one responded. Several of us had worked on the hole, but I was the last one to carve and that railroader had reported it to the guards. I stepped forward and said simply:

"I did it."

One of the guards asked something of the Russian lieutenant standing outside with more soldiers armed with rifles.

"*Davai.*"

It took only a second and I was outside on the ground. Small piles of gravel are often stored along German railroad tracks for repairing the tracks. The lieutenant was standing on one of those piles. He pointed to his men to take me to the end of the train and shoot me. I did not understand the words, but I understood his gestures. Three guards led me to the rear of the train, insulting me along the way. They seemed to enjoy the whole procedure. It was a boring job to guard a trainload of prisoners and this was a little action. When we arrived at the last car, they ordered me to turn around so they could shoot me in the back. I had no reaction. I was not afraid. "Go ahead," I said.

Then another thought came to me: You won't do it. You have to account for every man. The lieutenant yelled an order, and they pointed for me to go back to the other soldiers in front of our boxcar. The heavy sliding door was closed but not locked. They made a move indicating I should open the door and get back into the car. At that same moment, a couple of the soldiers started jabbing me with the butts of their rifles. I cried out to the men inside: "Help me open the door!"

The men were aware of what was happening outside, pushed the door open, grabbed my hands, and pulled me inside the car. The soldiers kept beating on me until I was out of their reach. Someone shut the door, *click!* and we were locked in again. Some of the men felt sorry for me. Others thought it was fair for what I had done. "Why did you have to enlarge that hole?" they complained.

I didn't care what they thought. I was hurting, mostly over my back, rear end, and hands. For a long time I did not say anything. I just moaned and groaned. I could not lie down on the hard plank floor as I had before, so I had to kneel or stand. One of the men who helped pull me inside the car had been beaten on his hand quite badly, and another on his arm. I apologized and thanked them for helping me get back into the car. It had been a terrible night, and the next day was not going to be much better. In the meantime, we moved. The train rolled for hours and then came to a stop again. Trains passed us on the next track over. We could see by looking through our hole that we moved in a southeasterly direction, which indicated we were not going toward home.

"How long do you think we have been in this car — two days, maybe three?" I asked of nobody in particular.

"We have finally arrived somewhere. I can see it is a big, busy railroad yard," replied a man with his eye to the hole.

A Continent Divided

Breslau. It was Breslau (Wrocław), the end of the line, the end of the European track size. Soon we would see wider Russian tracks and their long, much larger boxcars.

I tried to ignore the pain I felt. I could walk, and there was no outward sign of the beating I had taken except on my hand. I limped a little, but others did too after that many days in the boxcar.

The corpses of men who had died during the trip were in the last boxcar of our train. This was the reason we had heard boxcar doors opened and closed during the trip. It was the same car I stood beside when they were going to shoot me. I was right — the guards did have to account for every man, dead or alive.

Breslau was a prisoner of war camp with intercontinental railroad connections. It held thousands of prisoners. It was well organized. Prisoners received two meals a day: hot soup with a little substance and a slice of bread. We had a place to sleep; bunks were three tiers high to accommodate all the prisoners. Four of my men were still with me. We lost some at Sagan. We hung onto each other even more. Whatever had to be done, we did it together. The men were concerned about my condition. They gave me their coats to lie down on, and rolled mine up as a pillow. Their care for me was more than comforting. The pain seemed to diminish.

Breslau was a come-and-go camp. Trip after trip came in with old men, and really old ones, and young men who were still children, and every age in between. It was as though the entire male population of Germany was assembled here in Breslau — all stages of life, all physical conditions, all mentalities. Some were always on the lookout for something to eat, some word, some advantage, some hope. They did not know anything. All was hearsay and rumors. Some men lived on that and others just stared out into space. My mind warned me not to listen to rumors, though it felt so good to hear what I wanted to hear. I forced myself to face reality. They hadn't brought us here from all the old battlefields to send us home.

Here is where the east and the west meet, where European rails end. Here in Breslau, the Russian track begins leading east. As the Russian front came westward, so came the Russian railroad behind them. Years ago Germans going east changed the Russian tracks to German gauge for supply and transport, and for moving Russian prisoners of war to the west. Now the Russians were doing the same, only in reverse. They moved the tracks back to their gauge for transport and supply and to move train after train of German prisoners of war east. I felt compelled to let the others know what I had discovered. I said to the guys:

"They have assembled us here to ship us east. The question is only where? What kind of camp will we be sent to and for how long? They would not make all this effort to send us home in a few months. Let's not fool ourselves."

A hearsay story of World War I German prisoners of war in Russia came to mind. How cold it was, but the "freedom" they enjoyed in the camps! Some liked it so well they never went back home, settled in Russia, married, and started a new life and are still there. Maybe Russia is not so bad after all.

One of the guys got wind of the fact that one of the dishwashers was sick and they needed a new dishwasher. He explained to us, "I want to go for it because I will get a lot to eat from the kitchen in exchange for my work. Then I can save my bread ration and share it with the rest of you."

It sounded too good to be true. I asked him: "Have you observed the dishwashing process? The dishwasher starts out with a good-sized pan of hot water to wash the tin bowls of the men leaving the dining hall. Fortunately, the soup is very thin and nobody leaves anything in the tin bowls anyway, which helps with the cleaning process. The first twenty to fifty bowls make it through fairly clean, but after two hundred or more, it becomes only a symbolic act to move the bowls through the water. By then the dishwashing water has the color of the soup they served. There is not much difference in either the color or the substance, except that the soup served is fairly hot."

Some of the men giggled. They thought it was funny, but I hadn't meant it as a joke. I really felt it was a fact.

My thoughts went in that direction — or did I pray?

Thank you, Lord. We did not know what would be waiting for us, or what to expect. Let us receive it moment by moment. We prisoners would not be asked where we want to go, or what we want to do. Help us, Lord, to survive. The condition we are in right now is only temporary — what will be next? I trust you. *Please get us out of here!*

Train to Somewhere

Going East Our little troop was prepared to make the best of things. We watched for a trip being put together and decided to go for it. Trips were coming in from the west and trips were going out to the east. We were ready. It went fast. They herded a load of men together, and suddenly we were right in the middle of it, counted and counted again, and on our way. We knew about rows of five passing the Russian officer, and this was our railway ticket to somewhere. There was that first Russian word again; "*Davai, davai.*" It meant almost anything: come, go, stop, sit down, get up, keep going, emphasized by the proper motion of the hand. We got into a boxcar higher and bigger than our previous German "home." What a surprise to discover a bucket mounted to the floor in the corner with a hole in it — the toilet. It was a great improvement. Being the first ones in, we settled into the opposite corner hoping to get better air. Not knowing how crowded the car would be, we did know that whatever space we claimed in the beginning would be our territory for the rest of the trip. We settled down in our corner, ready for the "adventure" that lay before us, wondering what it would be.

We had time to think and to talk. We had lost two men. One we remembered so well. He was the one who "found" all of the potatoes for our cow-head feast. How long ago was that now? There were only three of us left from the original group: Franz Gielen, Rudi Strohbach, and me. We were on a first-name basis, our ranks left far behind. We were just men, stripped of all documents and belongings — with no identification. We had only our uniform, overcoat, cap, and boots. Traveling was pleasant. The days were comfortably warm and the nights not too cold. We must be going through the southern part of Russia. The atmosphere in the boxcar was relaxed. We were on our way to somewhere, come what may. The men liked to talk about the last days or last moments before being captured. It relieved their anxiety and justified their final actions. As I listened to the stories, I realized how lucky we had been to be taken prisoner without bloodshed and without losing a single man. Franz and Rudi told our story. A smile came when they told about our first hour of being prisoners, sitting in the pantry of the farmhouse eating the farmer's canned goods. They also told how the guards had beaten me up.

The *clickety-click* of the rolling train was soothing. It felt good to be going, knowing we would eventually get to some destination. Our little group loosened up with personal stories of our lives, our homes, families, and jobs. We had deep concerns about the fate of our loved ones. Would they know that we were still alive?

We had the right to write letters and receive mail as prisoners of war under international Red Cross agreements. Someone mentioned that American prisoners of war received parcels from America. They called them care packages. Another knew they had to release us within a certain time period after a war ends. We had all of the answers and they were always in our favor. We were fooling ourselves, but it gave us hope. Hope gave us faith, and faith gave us the courage to accept whatever might come. For now, there was only one reality: We were on a train in Russia going east, and they would not be taking us farther and farther into the country if they intended to send us home next month or even next year. Nobody wanted to talk about that.

Just a Break, but a Blessing The rhythm of the train's wheels changed. The *clickety-click* got slower and slower. Finally, we stopped. A stop made us more aware of our surroundings: the hard floor we sat and laid down on; the closed doors that imprisoned us; that we were prisoners. We heard the guards outside. Then came the squeak of boxcar doors opening. The *click* as they were unlocked from the outside and *"Davai"* as we opened the doors from the inside — a chore we gladly did. Outside! But was this the end of the trail? There was wide nothingness — prairie.

They ordered us to stay at a specified place along the train. We would be there for about an hour. Guards were posted on the embankment by the side of the tracks. The room between the cars and the guards was all ours. But we were outside walking on mother earth again — fresh air, sunshine. We felt almost free. I silently thanked the Russian in charge who let us out to enjoy the fresh air while waiting for the train to start up again. Some of the prisoners who spoke a little Russian, Polish, or Yugoslavian languages tried to find out from the guards where we were. The guards either didn't know or were not allowed to tell us. We were somewhere between the Oder and the Volga Rivers, but Russia is a big, wide-open country. We were going east, far away from our homeland. The order came to climb back in the boxcars — our "home," where we could sit, talk, lie down. We finally started rolling. The *clickety-click* made us comfortable again. Another day had passed.

Deeper and deeper into Russia we went.

Caucasus

Coat Collection With the stop-and-go traveling, how far we had gone into Russia was purely a guess. Our main direction was east and sometimes south. On one stop, the door opened. A sergeant followed by two soldiers entered, explained that we were headed into the Caucasus region and would no longer need our overcoats, then collected them and threw them out the door of the boxcar. With them went our mattresses, blankets, pillows. The coats were gone, the doors locked, and soon we were on our way again.

I had been in the Caucasus near the Terek River with the 13th Tank Division, in the fall of 1942. That same winter Stalingrad was recaptured by the Russian Army. I told those near me what I remembered of the area.

I told them there were beautiful green valleys where grapes and peaches and all kinds of fruit grew. It was surely a country where milk and honey flowed, and the people living there were friendly.

As I spoke, some other men came to our group to hear what I had to say. This is the story I told them.

Memories For about a year, I was assigned to the German Army Movie Outfit that produced instructional movies for training exercises. We were to be stationed with the 13th Tank Division by the Don River in the summer of 1942. Our goal was to make movies for training tank commanders and officers. Three points were emphasized: Coordination of Tanks and Infantry, Tanks and Artilleries, and Tanks and Technical Corps. Colonel Schmahl from the Special Tank Unit was in charge. I became his right-hand man. He gave me complete freedom to organize the cameramen. The colonel opened every door necessary for me to accomplish our goal. I was in my element organizing and producing movies. That had been the dream of my life — to be a movie director. The picture is the main element of a film. All other ingredients — directing, acting, makeup, script, costumes, props, and so on — are expressed through the picture. We had no script. Who could know how a battle would progress?

I assigned cameramen to different vehicles, and we talked over what we wanted to accomplish. Take any picture that might support the theme. Every morning I was present for the tactical instruction of the regiment commander, Colonel Burmeister, who gave an overview of each day's operation. I moved around freely in my assigned smaller tank to any spot I sensed might be a hot spot for pictures. I rolled right along behind the heavier tanks that did the shooting. Through steady radio-telephone communication, I always knew what was going on. I heard their target descriptions and was prepared for action.

In one situation the sun had just begun to go down. Slowly it turned dark. I was sitting between two of the big tanks. There was an antitank gun directly in front of us. I would not have recognized it. I heard over the radio one commander describing the target to the other one. Still I could not see it, but held the camera in the direction of the target and let it run. Grenades with flares came from the left and right — I hung onto the camera. There were some perfect shots. A big burst in the air ... an ammunition storage must have been hit. What a huge flare!

As night came, we assembled to form a fort. The tanks were parked in a wide circle with guns to the outside. Inside was ammunition for the guns, gasoline for the tanks, spare parts, and a motorized field kitchen that came in to supply the only hot meal of the day.

On my way back to the assembling area, I came upon a burning Russian tank. We had shot it earlier in the day during the tank battle. I stopped and took shots from a distance, then closer, and finally a close-up, which I felt would give a good sequence in later editing. It was a miracle the way it all came together.

As we went through the Kalmuck Steppe, we filmed the tanks as they worked together with the infantry. The foot soldiers followed the slow-moving tanks. Soldiers also rode lying on top of the tanks to the next village. They combed from house to house with tanks covering the men as they went.

The technical troops built a pontoon bridge for the tanks to cross a river. The camera crews took some amazing shots. We had our hearts in the project and risked our lives to get the most effective sequences.

I was excited talking about those times to the men. My heart was in those films. I considered it a great privilege to make moving pictures of the war — realistic pictures right out on the battlefield. I paused in telling my story. Questions came fast and furious:

"Did you finish your work?"
"What happened to the films?"
"Tell us the end of your story."

As I went on talking, I became completely absorbed with the happenings of those past days. I had exchanged my present circumstances for deeper, engraved memories.

I collected the films for our return to Berlin for developing and labeling. Colonel Schmahl arranged for me to have excerpts of the official regiment battle diaries. One of them was mentioned in the *Wehrmachtsbericht*.

Schmahl and I left our film troops and rushed back to Berlin. The colonel was an old fox, a World War I officer. Traveling from this southeast corner of Russia to Berlin, he always met someone from the old days who was helpful (hopping aboard a supply truck, a flight in a cargo plane, and so on).

The colonel looked at me with a grin, the ever-present monocle held tightly in his right eye as if to say, "Schuetz, we will make it home in no time." He wanted to stay and visit with old buddies at a makeshift officers club. But I pushed him to go back to the Army Film Unit Headquarters in Berlin. Those films were my babies. I had my heart in the project and the tank battles were still fresh in my mind. With Schmahl's support I had caught the principals of tank battle tactics and wanted to bring it all into focus with the films. "Colonel, let us go on." We ended up that day in the Führer's Headquarters. I got a good night's sleep and good meals in the guest house. The Führer was not around.

Colonel Schmahl arranged for a ride in the special train from Hauptquartier direct to Berlin. He apologized that a sleeper was not available to me, but arranged for first-class travel in the Courier Compartment. I was only a corporal.

In Berlin, I delivered the film for developing and used the time to study the regiment field diary. Later, reviewing the filmstrips, I was amazed at how excellent the material was. The men had done a great job! The drama of the battles shone forth from the film. I labeled every scene and created the finished films in my mind. Two days later I finished writing scripts for the three movies we were ordered to make.

It was now up to the colonel. He had to formulate commands that a tank commander would have given during the battles — terms I was not familiar with.

We had to return to our camera crews and to the same combat units to film fill-in scenes. That was impossible to do while battles were raging. We had to get the exact commands of the officer in charge so the tactical lessons for future tank commanders and officers would be correct.

My conversation with Schmahl was in the third person, the old army style of my active duty time, 1935–37. For example, "I beg Herr Colonel to have it arranged for Colonel and me to return to the front to film fill-in scenes." Schmahl liked this way of speaking, and I did, too. It put distance between the higher rank and me.

This time the colonel and I traveled by train. The closer we came to the front lines, the less comfortable were the railroad cars. It was third-class travel on wooden seats. I carried a little suitcase to use as a desk to make notes. We had daily travel rations and once in a while got hot soup from the Red Cross in larger railroad stations. Mostly we depended on cold rations we carried with us.

When we were ready for dinner on the train, I set my little suitcase in my lap and covered it with half a towel like a tablecloth. I got my cutting board out and a slice of bread and made an open sandwich. I ate it with a knife and fork. It was almost like home at the dining room table. Schmahl watched me, finally bursting out:

"Schuetz, that looks so gracious, the way you prepare your meal; you have to do it for me, too."

"Yes Colonel, I will, but with the Colonel's rations."

"Of course, of course."

I fixed his sandwich, but he did not have a knife and fork, so he had to eat with his hands.

Our relationship was very good — almost a friendship. We did not see eye to eye about the war and the Nazi Party. I was honest with Schmahl in our many conversations during our travels, sharing my thoughts about the mess Hitler had created since 1933. Schmahl was too intelligent not to see and maybe agree with some of my points. But he had great ambition to be a general. He used me to make those films, supporting me in every way to further his career. Schmahl highly recommended me to become an officer. He wanted me in the officers corps even though I would only be a lieutenant. Having no ambition to become an officer, I declined his offer. I was happy as a corporal. He respected my wishes and the subject was never brought up again.

Just a few weeks before I was taken prisoner, an unusual incident happened between Colonel Schmahl and me that showed the depth of our man-to-man relationship. It was on one of those not-quite-legal trips to Berlin to see my mother-in-law. I was at the train station in Charlottenburg waiting for a train back to Potsdam. In the dark I walked up and down on the platform to pass the time. I passed an officer and saluted. We recognized each other at the same moment. It was Schmahl. I exclaimed, "Colonel!"

"He responded: 'Schuetz.'"

We shook hands and Schmahl held on firmly. I saw by his insignia that he had not made general. Had he gained a broader perspective now that the war was coming to its terrible end? He did not say in words: Schuetz, how did you know it would come to this? His pride stopped him from saying the words. He showed me only a smile under the tightly kept monocle in his right eye and one hand on my shoulder. He inquired as to where I was stationed, and wanted to have me transferred to his outfit. He said he could use a radio operator like me. Our trains arrived. We departed in different directions. I sensed this surprise meeting had made his day. I never saw or heard from him again. I respected Schmahl. He was the prototype of German officers of the old order. We had worked together, each using the other one for different reasons. He wanted to be promoted. I was in love with creating films.

The camera crews were waiting for our return to the Caucasus foothills. Schmahl had organized the impossible. He got the last two seats on a Junker airplane into P'atigorsk. The city is surrounded by foothills of the Caucasus Mountains. I saw Elbrus and Kaspek as the plane approached from the northwest. What a sight! I had visited Switzerland when I was five years old and learned to love the mountains. I was often homesick for the Alps. And here the magnificent snow-capped peaks were contrasted with the green pastures of the valley below with its great orchards of fruit trees. Yes, here was a country flowing with milk and honey!

The camera crews were glad to see us again, for they were eager to go back to work. An invitation to have dinner with them was graciously extended. They had "confiscated" a five-gallon can of egg yolks. Someone made an omelet for me. It was heavy and later I did not feel too well. How good, though, was the warm reception.

Next day we went to our tank division at the Terek River. They had built a bridgehead on the south side of the river. A strong Russian tank unit was opposite them. An attack could come at any time. We needed shots of certain tank commanders to make the films seem real. I set two cameramen on each side of a tank as the commander gave orders to hit a target. The Russians must have noticed the activity around the tank. We heard the *ping*, as one grenade missed us to the left. We kept on filming. *Ping*— the next missed us to the right. The tank commander shouted: "We'd better move to another position. The next one will hit us for sure.

We took all necessary pictures to complete our task according to the scripts and were ready to go back behind the front lines. On the pontoon bridge, which was the only crossing over the river, we were required to wait as heavy traffic rolled toward us. One of the cameramen took pictures of the bridge and the crossing traffic just as an airplane dropped some bombs. Fortunately, they missed the bridge, but hit on our side of the river embankment and one of my men was wounded. His thigh was cut wide open with the bone sticking out. We loaded him onto one of our vehicles. I told the driver to rush to the other side as soon as the traffic stopped coming. The bridge had only one lane. I walked across, hoping to direct traffic. It was a miracle I got it stopped, our vehicle crossed, and we were back on the north side, not too far away from a field hospital.

We took him in, got him a bed, and had him tagged. He got some medication for his pain. I waited with him and talked to the surgeon in charge, who promised our man would be the next one in surgery. Would they have to amputate his leg? I stayed with him to encourage him. He gave me the name and address of his wife. They had just been married for a couple of months. I promised to write or call her since Berlin was his home town. A male nurse came and rolled him into the surgery room of the makeshift hospital that was set up in an old factory building. I had done all I could do, and I left in peace.

Our vehicles and men would be loaded on a freight train headed for Berlin. Schmahl organized the trip back, and between trucks, trains, and a stint on a cargo plane, then back on the train again, we made it to Berlin.

I reported to the Film Unit and told them of the serious wounding of one of the men. I called his wife and told her about what had happened. As gently as possible, I prepared her for the possibility that her husband might lose a leg.

While the film was being developed, I made all the other preparations. I got assigned to a branch office in Paris where there was a film editor on staff. They could take care of making copies and give me all the support I needed and couldn't get in Berlin.

In Paris I met the cutter, Peter Paris. We clicked together from the first moment we met. He did not mind working hard. We spent days and some nights editing the material according to the script. When we found another film clip that expressed even better the battle scenes, we used it. Peter was continually surprised at how well I knew the material. Sometimes we searched for hours for a scene I knew existed that needed to be edited into the film. We always found it.

I returned to Berlin with three films, complete with sound tracks but no dialogue. That should be synchronized in Berlin where a better sound studio was available.

I was ordered to report to the chief of our unit. He had just received the tag of my wounded cameraman marked, "Dead on Arrival" at the field hospital, complete with unit number and date. What a blow that was to me! The major accused me of being a liar and said I had tried to cover up the man's death.

How could I defend myself? I had no witness. When I saw the tag, correctly filled out with "leg injury," and then written across, "Dead on Arrival," I could see how it might have happened. In a field hospital, wounded after wounded were cared for under tense conditions — surgery after surgery. Maybe the wound was more severe than I realized and he had lost too much blood already. At the field hospital it made no difference if he died on the operating table or was dead on arrival. It saved a lot of paperwork they didn't have time for anyway. I took the blame. I was there, I had done what I could, I was at peace with the situation.

I felt sorry for the young bride who was now a widow. I called her to explain the situation in the field hospital. I don't know if she believed me. The news was a blow to both of us.

Word spread about the films. I showed them to Schmahl and read the dialogue we had worked out many weeks before. He set up another showing of the films and said I should speak the dialogue as I had done earlier. The day of the film premiere arrived. Three generals with their staffs, another colonel, and the commander of the tank officer training school were there. I had not known about the competition between the commander of the school and Schmahl, who would be the next general-level officer.

The lights in the projection room dimmed. I sat in the rear at a desk with the script before me, ready to speak the dialogue. The film began to show on the screen. It started with a staff meeting and a map of the front lines. One officer was explaining the situation at the front when the film blended into action with the tanks. My voice came out of the speaker behind the screen, clear and solid. I was in my element. There was the product! It was good — thanks to all who had made it possible. The soldiers in the tanks on the battlefield, the men who took the pictures, everybody had given their best. One had given his life. When a movie is completed, the director gets most of the credit, but in reality it is the teamwork and cooperation working together that brings about the results.

The show was a success. One of the generals shook my hand and congratulated me. I thanked the general, but pointed to Colonel Schmahl, who had supported the work in every way and gave his excellent advice wherever it was needed. The colonel of the Tank Officer Training School wanted the half-completed films right away. He wanted to show them to the present class of new tank officers. I objected because the films were not completed — no words, no text. It made no sense to show the pictures with the sound track, but without the text that brings it alive. We lost. The films went with the school commander and never came back.

That night in March of 1945, when Colonel Schmahl and I both happened to be at the railroad station in Charlottenburg, I saw he had lost out. He was still a colonel. The war had not turned out as he had hoped. I was still a corporal looking forward to the end of the war soon. I lived moment by moment with tongue in cheek, saying: "Enjoy the war, the peace will be terrible!"

Uncertain Directions There was silence in the boxcar. The men thought about the story I had told them. It had turned dark without our noticing it. We had not had a meal since morning, a piece of bread and some water. I thought to myself, Why did I tell them all this? I got carried away. I just wanted to tell them how well the people in the Caucasus region treated us when we were there.

As the train rolled along, we lost all sense of direction. Not until the next morning did we determine that we were headed north again. It was not easy to know which way the train was going. The Russian railroad tracks ran straight for miles and miles with sometimes only a light turn into another direction. It was certain that we were going mainly in an easterly direction. Our best navigating took place at sunrise or sunset; recognizing east and west made it easy to determine north or south. Our direction occasionally changed during the day and sometimes during the night, so our efforts were open to all kinds of discussion and guesswork. At least it helped to while away the long hours.

Some of the men separated themselves and brooded quite a bit. They did not take part in our discussions or listen to the stories of others. Those were the ones who were crushed, beaten down in spirit, all hope gone, with no more illusions. Their lives, their hopes, their future had depended on the Nazis and Hitler, and Dr. Goebbels' rhetoric and promises on the one hand and his demands on the other. Was there no more to life than those twelve years of the promised thousand-year Reich? Where did Hitler get the idea of the thousand-year Reich anyway? Had he tried to imitate Christ's coming and reigning over the earth for a thousand years?

Most of us wanted to survive. We had hope — hope for the days to come, hope that we would make it and return home someday. With hope one does not have to have a final date. Real hope never ends. It is an inner force that sustains us to survive and carry on, to keep on hoping. It is a spiritual gift. Oh, blessed hope!

The day we detected our movement to the north and east, those who had hope looked at me. Had I not said that the Caucasus Mountains were in the south of Russia? I remained silent. There was nothing I could say.

We must have been in the boxcar for seven days. Some insisted it was at least nine. It was too long. One time we were allowed out of the boxcar in the sunlight for about an hour.

Saratov (Zorotov)

Arrival The train came to a stop. What were the noises we thought we heard: automobiles, streetcars? The guards unlocked the doors after long hours of waiting. It took an effort to jump to the ground after all those days in the car. The long hours and days had weakened us. Had we arrived at our destination? This was certainly not the Caucasus. There were no mountains to be seen around us. It looked more like a flat expanse of countryside. A prisoner of war camp was right next to the railroad tracks. Word spread around that this was Saratov. Where is Saratov located in Russia? We waited in rows of five beside our cars to be counted. There were fifty men per car. Five must be a magic number to the Russians: rows of five, fifty men per car, production goals in five-year increments. Five was also an easy figure to multiply by.

Word spread around that Saratov is on the Volga to the north of Stalingrad (now Volgograd). Prisoners always needed to know something about everything, even if it was not true. This time it was right — this was Saratov.

As we marched into the camp, other prisoners watched. Their expressions said we looked mighty pitiful. All those days in the boxcars with little food and no bath had taken their toll. Since Stahnsdorf, we had been en route for about six to eight weeks. But we had made it. We had finally arrived at a destination. As we mingled with the "local" prisoners, we had many questions: "How is the food?" "What kind of work?" "How many men in the camp?" "Are there other camps around in the vicinity?" All we longed to know.

It was afternoon. The sun was our timekeeper now.

During normal times, if someone asked the time of day, we checked our watches. In olden days, one got out his pocket watch as my father used to do. It was a beautiful, flat pocket watch with a spring lid to protect the glass. He took it out of his vest and opened the spring lid, looking so distinguished. While eating breakfast at home, the watch lay on the table with the lid open right next to him. Later, during the war, I told my father if I inherited anything I hoped it would be that watch. After Waldemar's death, he assured me I would own it someday. When I went to Düsseldorf to father's funeral and to take care of his belongings, I asked if anyone had found his pocket watch. No. Father's dentist, who had identified him as Walther Schütz, said I should keep my father in my memory, that I should not go to his viewing. Now in the prisoner of war camp, I didn't need my father's watch. I had the sun!

The Garden of Eden As we strolled around the camp it was hard to believe our eyes. Was what we saw a reality? The camp seemed to be a flower bed with barracks scattered around in it enclosed by barbed wire. The story went that the Russian commander had found a prisoner who was a gardener. This man was kept for only one job in the camp: to start a flower garden and take care of it. He collected the seeds and built a makeshift greenhouse to start early seedlings for planting outside at the right time. There were many different varieties of flowers blooming from early spring until late in the fall. The camp was wedged between the railroad tracks and a main road leading to somewhere, with streetcar tracks running along the camp fence. We noticed that the passengers in the streetcars faced the camp side to see this paradise of flowers. What a joy they were for many of us who had an eye for beauty.

We hadn't eaten, but didn't feel hungry. So many impressions were coming at us from so many different directions. It was exciting. After what we went through, this was to us the Garden of Eden.

"Saratov Special" Standing around, just watching, we noticed a group was forming in rows of five. Word spread fast. It was a food line. To the dining hall we went. A bowl of hot soup with a little something solid in it and a slice of bread — a good start. There was good news after the meal — to the bathhouse for delousing. We walked out of the camp to the streetcar stop by the gate. An empty streetcar came along reserved for prisoners. I could hardly believe it. We were riding in a special streetcar that civilians could not jump on. Some tried it, but the guards pushed them away. They left cursing and shaking a raised fist. We sat inside, comfortably riding in style.

Banja The ride on the streetcar was long. We finally came from the outskirts of Saratov into the inner city, and to our destination: *Banja* (bathhouse) #3. As we entered the building the warm, steaming air filled our nostrils. It smelled so clean. We waited in the hallway while the one in charge arranged for the *vojeno plenys* (prisoners of war). *Vojeno plenys* was our official title from then on. Finally we went into a room and were ordered to undress and put our belongings on a coat hanger. We stood there plain naked. The coat hangers went into another room with heat coils in the floor. The temperature should be so high the lice in our garments would be killed. In the bathhouse we learned the bathing procedure. We grabbed a wash pan and a glob that looked like grease or wagon fat. We filled the wash pans with water and wiped the "soap" on our bodies. I put the stinking stuff right on my chest. It stuck to my skin like glue. That freed my hands to fill the pan with water. How would I clean my whole body with a pan of water? Wasn't that the purpose of the "*Banja*?" I took the glob of "soap" from my chest and smeared it on a wooden bench, then dumped the pan of warm water over myself. It felt so good that I repeated it right away. Now that I was wet, I picked up the soap and smeared it all over my body. We helped each other in doing our backs. It was a smeary mess and smelled like wheel grease. I tried to wash it off like in a shower with one bowl of water after the other. But the stuff stuck. Finally, with water and plenty of rubbing it came off the front of our bodies, and we cleaned each other's backs.

In the bathhouse we learned the bathing procedure.

God must have had a purpose when He created man to be unable to reach every part of his own body. Maybe that was the reason that He made a helper for Adam — to scratch his back.

The end result was what counted. We did feel cleaner than when we came into "*Banja #3.*" Since our clothes had to be in the delousing process for a certain length of time, in waiting around we dried off naturally.

Everybody miraculously was able to find his own wear. The warmed-up uniforms felt pleasant on our bodies.

Guards came in, "*Davai, davai,*" rows of five. We were counted, nobody was missing. "*Davai*" outside to the streetcar for our ride back to camp?

No Round Trip No! Our guards had different orders. We got into formation and marched in the opposite direction. It had by then grown dark. No sun, no direction, and we could not stop to search for the North Star. We just walked. There were hardly any civilians on the city street or in the suburbs of Saratov. The warm clothes on our bodies made us sweat.

I was tired, and had been tired for a long time; those weeks in the boxcars with not enough to eat, the beating — then warm bathing, and now walking, walking, no direction, not knowing how much further. No goal, no zeal. I wished that I could just lie down and not think at all for a while. We were a herd of human beings, walking; I had to keep walking, too. Keep going, keep going. It must all come to an end, and soon. And it did.

"*Stoy!*" (Stop!) This is it!

The night was very dark — no moonlight, no street lights. We could make out a high wooden fence with barbed wire on top. One of the guards rattled the big gate, but it was locked. He said something in Russian. It sounded like cursing. There was a commotion among the guards. We stood and waited, and waited. It was almost worse than walking. How we yearned to just lie down, stretch out and rest, get a good night's sleep and not care what the next day would bring.

One of the guards returned with the key, opened the gate, and we walked in. Before us was a two-story wooden building. We assumed that it was used for prisoners before. There was no light in the yard and no light inside the building. We were herded into a room to the right of a small hallway. As we groped around, we made out bunks: four in a group, mounted to two center posts, one bunk to the left and one to the right, with the same arrangement above. I grabbed an upper one, climbed up, and stretched out on the bare planks. In a short time we had settled down without much conversation and most went sound asleep.

Night Visitors I was half asleep when a lot of commotion aroused me. I did not want to be disturbed. I barely made out men sitting up on their bunks, others standing and walking the floor. What had happened that they did not sleep?

The warm smell of fresh, sweaty human flesh had attracted bedbugs. They came out from somewhere in large numbers. They must have been starved for years, the way they came after the men. None seemed to be on my own body. Not yet, anyway! We got no sleep the rest of that night. There was no light inside the building, and no light in the yard or in the surrounding area. Sunrise was a release from the darkness. The guards let us out of the building and we explored the camp. There were no lightbulbs in the sockets. Electricity had not even been hooked up. We found a latrine, but the water was not connected. This place had been stripped of everything. The camp must have been a prison camp for Russian civilians and abandoned when the Germans got close to Saratov in the battles around Stalingrad.

Home Sweet Home Was this to be our home? The rest room and the malfunctioning washroom we had already visited. There was not much more to explore except for a small house nearby: the latrine. It was locked. The room where we had spent the first night was much larger than we had thought. It ran the entire length of the building. As the bunk room was to the right of the hallway, straight ahead was the dining hall. To the left was the kitchen that was without any equipment and left in a state of destruction. In one corner lay a pile of broken bricks where a stove had been hooked up. Someone evidently had a use for it and tore it out. From the dining room a door led to the rear of the building. There was an open stairway leading to an upper room that took almost the whole upstairs. On the landing of the stairs we could get a view of the Volga River in the distance. It was quite a sight. The Volga was fairly wide at that point and the water ran peacefully southward. Across the Volga we could see forests near the river and then open land behind. Farther south was a long steel bridge crossing the water.

The sleeping room on the upper floor contained empty bunks and had more windows than the room downstairs where we had spent the first night. It had windows on three sides, but they did not open. They were not windows at all, just square glass in the wall to let light in. From the outside the windows on the ground level were like mirrors. They reflected images only in black and white because they were so dirty. Everything around the camp was colorless, different shades of gray. It was sad. If any chance came to pick a bunk my choice would be one in the upper room. The inconvenience of climbing the stairs, which were fairly steep, every time you had to go to the dining room, washroom, or latrine was not enough to deter me. The view over the river and the trees on the other side made that inconvenience worthwhile. The Volga seemed to be a mile wide. A mile of wide open space, and beyond. That is Russia's infinite openness. Here I understood what it meant.

Back in Berlin when I returned to label the film materials, I was invited to a friend of my mother-in-law's, an older lady. She had been given the nickname "Lion." She was tall and majestic. She had immigrated from Kiev after World War I and lived all those years in Berlin, but still had a strong Russian accent. I told her about some of my impressions when we went eastward engaged in tank battles without seeing any trees, and the sun shining from sunrise to sunset with no shade. As far as the eye could see, horizon, just horizon. The Lion saw her homeland, the Ukraine, in my story and burst out with, "Oh, Russia's infinite openness."

My reaction then was: "What is so exciting about it?" Now I got a glimpse of that excitement, sitting on those stairs letting my eyes wander to the river, over the waters to the bank on the other side, the forests, the open land beyond, and only guessing at the horizon. I could then forget the high wooden fence and the barbed wire of the camp. This is Russia!

... But Here Are the Facts The weather was perfect. Sunshine all day, warm, so we sat outside on those rough-built benches and visited and talked and listened, got tired of one group and moved on to another. You heard the same ifs ... and buts ... and whens ... in reality, nobody knew anything for sure. Reality was no water, no food.

The guards managed to get some cans of water, German milk cans. They were a little banged up and the lids were missing, but they were made of heavy metal that kept the water fairly cool. At least we had something to drink. We walked around to groups of men listening to what they talked about. "Hungry!" "Eating!" It became obvious the less we had to eat, the more we talked about food. It seemed to quiet our hunger. Our stomachs shrank in size and our bodies lived off the stored reserves in our system. Our last meal had been soup and a slice of bread the afternoon we arrived in Saratov.

Who Comes to Dinner Tonight? As evening drew closer, we made plans to sleep outside away from the bedbugs. But as it got darker the guards, very young, almost afraid but friendly, wanted to be sure we were all inside the building in that downstairs room just like the night before. This time we knew what to expect. The visitors came again. I got bit, and the spot swelled up and made a reddish bump on my skin. It was nothing compared to some of the other men, who really suffered with swollen bites all over their faces. It would be like this every night!

Our two milk cans were filled with fresh water that morning. The two men who went with the guards to fill the cans scouted around outside the fence and discovered a sawmill to the north. We had also discovered the walls of our building were insulated with sawdust, which is cheap and plentiful around a mill. Those critters had crawled into the sawdust to live on whatever they could. What a feast that first night when eighty warm, sweaty bodies moved in! They passed the word on to each other: fresh meat outside. They seemed to prefer some guys more than others. I was one of the lucky ones. Sometimes I was left out all together, and other times I became part of the menu just like the other men.

I looked forward to being outside in the sun, getting a drink of water to drown out that funny feeling in my stomach. Groups of men spread out all over the yard. We continued walking from group to group listening and talking. Sometimes we'd come upon a lonely man and talk man-to-man about personal things.

Talk About It The main theme was mostly about food. We exchanged recipes and listened to how the wife of an older prisoner baked a cake or the mother of a younger one prepared a meal. Everyone had a big roast at least every Sunday. They patted those roasts on the table of their memories and dreamed about how many eggs it took to make a cake, until someone said:

"If I had just one bite to eat of what we talk about, I'd be happy."

This brought us back to reality, and with that reality we were called to stand in line. A Russian "authority" must have finally thought about feeding the prisoners. The food request had to go through official channels, and the bureaucracy in Russia is worse than in other countries. Someone found some kind of food storage. It was passed down to us, half a handful each of solid, dried, aged dark bread in one-inch-square cubes — our ration for the day. The cubes were as hard as rocks. One could easily break a tooth chewing on them. I put each piece in my mouth to dissolve with my saliva.

It was just the opposite of the way Tante Else had trained her sons to chew the soup when there was nothing there to chew. It kept me busy, eating my bread cubes with a swallow of water in between. I saved some pieces in that linen sack the Kalmuck sergeant had given me on our march to Sagan. It was full of good bread then. Those little cubes did not compare to the original contents. I burped and my stomach said, What is this you sent down to me as my first meal in two days?

The little cubes turned out to be our "daily bread" for quite some time. At night we slept in the bedbugs' quarters and in the daytime told stories and listened to others' stories. Young prisoners drafted into the military from school told about their experiences over and over. Their stories were mostly about the last moments of the war before being captured by the Russians. Friends were killed in the encounter, leaders were lost, everything in their world collapsed. It was healing for them to talk about it until they could come to terms with the experience. It was their therapy. The older prisoners talked more about their home life, their families. Some colored their stories. It made them feel good. It was therapy for them, too. Most of their past would be gone now. They would have to start all over again if they ever made it home.

Three Left Over As mentioned earlier, three men were left from our original troop. Franz Gielen, an engineer with the Siemen's AG, Rudi Strohbach, a specialist in armament production, and me. We sat together and talked about the experiences we had lived through. They went back to our capture that Sunday afternoon when we ate the canned food in the farmer's pantry. They confessed to watching me closer than the Russians, suspecting I would try to escape without them. We expressed how glad we were to still be together, encouraging each other and taking whatever might come. The Russians would have to free us someday.

As the days went by, we got our milk cans filled with water more frequently. The daily bread rations became routine. One day I was able to sneak some water for washing myself. I learned from a Ukrainian traveling with our tank unit as a handyman, interpreter, organizer, and scout that you could sip a bit of water to flush your mouth, letting it flow slowly out of your mouth to wash your hands. You could let a second sip of water flow carefully into your tightly cupped hands and then bring your hands up to wash your face. I tried it, and it worked. I felt refreshed. I looked forward every morning to this "bathing" procedure.

Nothing to Do There were stories, stories, and more stories. After a time they became boring. The worst thing was we had nothing to do — no tools, no equipment, no plan, no schedule, no goal, and not much to eat. It drained us. Some of the prisoners claimed to be former officers. They tried to be in charge when there was nothing to be in charge of. Day after day passed uneventfully. We got sick and tired of sitting around and longed for something to do, any kind of work. We wanted to get out and be productive.

Günther As a group of new prisoners came into the camp, I met a young man who wore the uniform of the medical corps. Günther was the same rank as my brother Waldemar when I saw him that last time. Waldemar became lieutenant —*unterarzt*— as the campaign in Russia began. Günther was drafted just before finishing his final medical exam. We struck it off instantly. He was ordered to take care of the sick, which made him our physician. Even without his medical license, he was trusted and respected as someone who tried to help even with the meager supplies on hand. When we had time to visit, we shared memories of music, literature, travel. We always had something to talk about other than prison life and its routine bitching. I looked forward to spending time with him. Our relationship grew into a real friendship.

"Budit" (It Will Be) One glorious day a Russian in uniform came into the camp. He was a captain, maybe. Rank did not matter. He told us we would be getting three servings of soup with bread a day and *kasha* at the noon meal. He could have asked us to do anything and we would have done it. He was the first officer that had come into the camp and talked to us. He talked like someone with authority. He promised regular food! Then he asked in German if anyone spoke Russian. One fellow whom we had hardly noticed before answered the captain in fluent Russian. He was shy and always looked pale. He would act as interpreter and overseer for the camp. I found out later he was Polish. He had learned the language when Poland was occupied by the Russians. When the Germans came to Poland, he was drafted in the German Army. The Poles hate Russians and don't like Germans either. He was not quite as fluent in German as Russian, but we now had someone who could communicate with the Russians and tell us what they were planning. The Russian commander lifted our spirits just by his appearance and authority. He asked for a plumber to repair the waterline to the camp. He brought pipes, tools, whatever was needed to get water into the camp. Our plumber worked for two days to get us that precious running water. We had forgotten when we last had running water. Yes, it was in the *Banja*, the bathhouse, a long time ago.

Oh, blessed running water!

Our interpreter called the Russian commander *Natchalnik* (boss). We thought he might not even be an officer. What did it matter? He had brought us hope.

The *Natchalnik* was very clever. He knew how to handle us. He was trained for a job like this. On his daily visits we lined up in formation and he stood in front and asked what complaints we had. He heard everything. Nothing shook him. He acted like he expected those complaints and had an answer for everything. We wanted regular food. We were still on the dried cubes of bread.

"*Budit* [It will be]. You will have three servings of hot soup a day with bread and *kasha*. If you work, you will get plenty to eat. No work, no bread."

"How about mail, to write home?"

"*Budit*, you will have postcards to write home. The better you work, the more cards you will be able to write home."

"How about a bath, soap? Will be able to wash our clothes?"

"How about thread and a needle to fix our torn uniforms?"

He had an encouraging answer for each question. Everything was *Budit*. I think he believed it himself the moment he said it. What would be the reality of his promises? We would wait and see.

Then came an urgent question:

"What about bedbugs and lice in the building?"

This was his answer:

"The Germans brought the bedbugs and lice to Russia."

It was the first time we all laughed aloud, followed by a lot of sarcastic remarks. It was better he did not understand.

A prisoner who claimed to be a former German captain took charge in a diplomatic way and did a good job of organizing and keeping order. We were in need of someone in authority. Just sitting around listening to all of the stories and theories was depressing.

One "Budit" Turned into Reality On one of his visits, the *Natchalnik* asked for a bricklayer. He had gathered a big pot, some cement, a stack of bricks, a makeshift trowel, and some fieldstones. The bricklayer was prepared to do a lot of improvising to build a cooking stove in the kitchen. Just hearing about the cooking facility being built made our stomachs dance for joy. It took a couple more days for the mortar to dry before a fire could be built under the pot. He rounded up soup bowls, spoons, pans, and kitchen utensils for our new kitchen. Above all, we needed a cook. We were grateful to have running water in our kitchen already.

Hot Soup That first night we arrived at camp on our march from the *banja*, we had not noticed the one-story building outside the gate to the left of the guardhouse. This building was the magazine, the food storage supply house for the camp. One day came the now-familiar "*Davai, davai*." Helpers were needed and those men hanging around the gate went to the magazine to haul supplies from the main warehouse. That evening the camp was full of stories by those guys who had brought in the supplies: bread, potatoes, oil, flour, grits, salt, butter, and meat. It took two more days for our cook, a former baker, to learn how to prepare a tasty soup. There were just enough tin bowls to feed twenty men in one sitting. With the soup, we got a piece of fresh baked bread. No more dry bread! It was our first hot meal in how long?

We did not have much time to enjoy our hot meal. There were others waiting and it was hurry, hurry, get out. I almost fainted trying to gulp the first hot soup down. I saved the bread 'til later, eating it slowly. The meals were served in that manner for quite a few days until more tin bowls became available and we could fill the dining hall and sit down — not being rushed by the guys waiting behind us.

It was a happy day.

The Sawmill

A Blessing We added new words to our Russian language encounters. "*Davai, robota.*" (Come, go to work.) We were divided into different work brigades. We were finally going outside our tall wooden fence. Just getting outside made us more alive and hopeful. After work there was something to talk about, the experiences of the day. Going to work was a blessing.

The talk about the sawmill was right. It was a good-sized mill to the north adjacent to our camp. Actually, the camp was a part of the sawmill. It had probably been built for Russian civilian prisoners who worked at the mill. We *vojeno plenys* (prisoners of war), had to bring the mill back into operation. Mechanics worked on the machinery and the saws. We began to understand how the mill had worked. Log rafts came down the Volga from the forests in the north. The logs were transported on a long conveyor to the top of the embankment and fell into the mill pond. Here the logs were sorted by length and size and brought to the big saw for cutting.

The First Job Assignment My first job was to clean out the mill pond where the floating logs had lost their bark. The sawmill must have stopped operating during the war, or maybe before. It had been neglected for many years. Our assignment was to dig out the layers of bark that had accumulated over a long period of time. Some of us got shovels, others paired up and got a *nasilki*, a contraption similar to the travois, used to move material before the wheel was invented. A platform about thirty inches square and bordered by one-by-eights on three sides is mounted on two sticks that serve as handles for two men to carry. The shoveler filled it with bark and the carriers dumped it at the designated spot by holding the open side down and lifting the bordered side so that the load slid off. And so it went, load after load. To make the job more interesting, the shovelers and carriers traded off. It was a repetitious job. At the end of a day, we saw how little we had taken out of that huge basin. It was going to be a long, boring job.

In time we removed most of the top layer, which was well dried. Then came the muddy, still-moist layer, which was heavier to carry and harder to dig out.

The whole job lasted for months and we never did clean the basin completely. A front-end loader would have accomplished it in a day or two.

The Menu Our camp life developed a routine. We got up early, washed with fresh, cold running water, had our morning meal of nearly a pint of hot water soup and a piece of bread, and between 7:00 and 7:30 A.M. walked out to our assigned job sites. Some men were transported by truck to faraway factories, always with a civilian guard. The sawmill brigade was the last to leave. We took three minutes to walk to our job site. The close-by work brigades came in at noon for lunch — again, hot water soup, a piece of bread, and a small portion of *kasha*. It was made out of oats, but could be anything else — potatoes, grits, barley, lentils, and one time even peas. If we arrived early at the dining hall, there was time for a nap before going back at one o'clock. We had a strict eight-hour working day, returning at 5:00 P.M.

Once in a while we got some *makhorka*, a little two-inch-square package of rough-cut tobacco made from the stems of the tobacco plant. Those who still had pipes enjoyed this strong tobacco. Where there is a demand, there is always a clever entrepreneur. Hand-carved pipes started appearing that were traded for soup, bread, tobacco, or anything of value. The guys on faraway work brigades, who did not come in for the noon meal, got two soups and bread (lunch and dinner), so they usually had something to trade, and the bartering began.

Improvements The factory work brigades smuggled in supplies that made us all more comfortable. We "got" light bulbs, faucets, and a shower head. We built a shower in the washhouse. It put out only cold water. So what — a shower! We "got" wire for lighting in the washroom and latrine.

Big, bright lights along the fence lit up the camp yard so the guards in their towers could watch any movement during the night, but regular lightbulbs were always in demand. If a Russian guard needed a bulb either for home, or his barracks, or to sell at the bazaar, he came inside the camp and took it. The *vojeno plenys* would replace it again. We had to bring everything through the guard at the gate. He checked us sometimes to see if we carried any contraband. This checking was only a show in case an officer happened to be present. If they found anything on a prisoner, it was confiscated and a report written to some official. No one gained. Most of the time the guards "overlooked" the goods and picked up what they wanted later. They called it *tsap-tsarap* (stealing). They did it to us, we did it to them — or more precisely, to their factories. It came out even — a very beneficial system for all.

Love Story We did not bring anything to the camp from the sawmill except firewood for the kitchen because that place was in need of everything. Between the mill pond and the sawmill, a bridge was built like an overhanging balcony. The man who selected logs stood on this bridge to bring the right log into the saw. One morning, as we came to our usual spot for our bark-moving brigade, a *magda*, a girl in her early twenties, seemed to be in charge of the work. She pointed to indicate that one man should work underneath the bridge and throw the accumulated bark into the open to be picked up. I volunteered. Nobody else wanted the job. I grabbed a spade and crawled on top of the dry bark underneath the bridge. There was not enough room to work comfortably, so I started along the edge next to the bridge. It was hard work and I made little progress. It was summertime. The days got hot. If I worked hard in the beginning, in a short time I would be in the shade under the bridge. The labor was not as hard anymore and the deeper in the pile I dug, the easier it was. The bark was fine and thinner, and not as twisted. I began to see it as a physical workout and it became fun — not hard at all. How we look at a situation makes all the difference in our attitude.

One day, when I had returned from our lunch break to my work place, the magda called:

"*Komrad, davai, komrad.*"

It took me a moment to realize she was calling me. I came out from underneath the bridge and climbed on the heap I had shoveled out. "*Davai,*" she said, and with this she gave me a big, cooked potato in the skin, and salt, plus a good chunk of bread that was bigger than what we received in the camp. This was for me, she said.

"*Spasibo.*" (Thank you.)

It was all I could say to express my appreciation and surprise. I went back under the bridge. What a wonderful gift! I ate the potato right away, and I put the bread with the salt pebbles in my linen sack and hid it under my shirt and jacket that I removed in the heat of the day. Lucky me! I worked twice as hard after that. Later in the evening as I told Günther, our "doctor," about it, he said in his humorous way with a big smile, "Hansarmin, she loves you."

We both had a good laugh. I offered to share the bread with Günther, but he declined. "You worked hard for that bread and you deserve it. I have enough to eat."

He lived with the officers upstairs and got better food to eat than we did.

It Comes, It Goes Life behind the walls became more and more routine. We had to keep our hair really short — bald. Body hair was shaved once in a while to reduce breeding places for lice. We all looked alike with our bald heads. To be different I grew a goatee, a rich, red blonde color. My hair was always dark blonde. I must have inherited the reddish blonde from my father. I often got compliments on my goatee and bartered two portions of bread for a comb to keep it neat. I could feel it more than see it since no mirrors were in the camp. Our camp barber was kept busy cutting off our hair. He trimmed my goatee neatly with every haircut.

Our Russian *Natchalnik* was replaced by a real army captain who insisted on being called "Commandant." Every evening there was roll call. The commandant went through the lines and looked us over. When he came to me he said something in Russian to the interpreter, who turned to me:

"You have to shave the goatee off."

"Why?"

"The commandant says you look like a saint; the goatee must come off."

It was three or four days before the men realized my goatee was gone. Even Günther, who saw me every day, didn't notice it right away. When he did, he said:

"What happened to your goatee?"

"I had it shaved off four days ago."

He could not believe he had not noticed it before. Was it the constant undernourishment that weakened us, or the whole atmosphere we lived in that stifled our observation abilities?

Cranking Up the Mill It was a joyful excitement for the Russians when the sawmill opened and a source of satisfaction for us *vojeno plenys*. After the first initial runs, the mill ran full steam. Soon a second shift was started — the day shift from 8:00 to 5:00, the night shift from 5:00 to 1:30 A.M.

Another shift was soon needed for the hours between 10:00 at night and 6:30 in the morning. That shift was for me. It would be different. It would get me out of my boring daytime work routine. A little before 10:00 P.M., the six men on this special night shift were called out; all the others had to be in their bunks.

Our job was to stack the freshly cut boards. The boards had to be packed on little wagonettes with lath in between. The one-by-sixes and one-by-eights then went into the kiln to dry. We worked in teams of two. The wagonettes were made of angle iron mounted on small steel wheels that ran on tracks like a railroad. We were the moving power. When the wagonettes were loaded, we only pushed our cargo into one of the many kiln chambers, and when dry, someone else pulled them out the other side.

Midnight Dreams My partner was about my size. He was a farm boy from East Prussia. My father was born in that part of Germany, as well as my grandfather who worked for the railroad. My teammate and I had a good rapport from the first. We put our wagonettes in place quickly about four feet apart. As we learned the operation, we did well and didn't mind the hard work.

The warm summer nights were beautiful. No "*Davai, davai,*" either, to bother us. We had two Yugoslavians in our brigade of six. One was a tall fellow who was perhaps the strongest of us all. He spoke German, Russian, and Yugoslavian lingo. He acted as our leader because he could communicate to both sides.

When one of the wagonette loads would not move on the tracks because of a lack of grease or bad alignment, or for whatever reason, the Yugoslavian would start cussing in German or Russian — words I had never heard. A chill would run down our spines and must have made us coordinate our pushing, because the wagonette slowly began to move. One time even the cursing did not help. We were stuck. Our foreman brought us a *lomb*, a heavy crowbar, and with our united effort at pushing, we moved the load ahead inch by inch. We became experienced loaders and movers, but discovered the hard-moving wagonettes were always at night. We began trying out each wagonette before setting it on the tracks. By using our experience and our heads, the Yugoslavian didn't have to cuss anymore.

Often under a full moon I thought about Annemie and Hans. They could see this same moon. How I wished we could have talked together over this "moon connection," to let them know I was alive here on the Volga River, that I did my best at my work and was experiencing a certain satisfaction. We got sentimental during those nights. Time went fast. It felt like we were through almost before we began. At 2:00 in the morning, we had a thirty-minute break halfway to our 6:30 quitting time.

A Pleasant Visitor On one of our breaks, a real boss came to the sawmill. He wore a Russian uniform without insignia. It looked like it had been left over from the war. I had the impression he wore it to show his authority. He sat with us, offering each of us a *papirosi*, those Russian cigarettes with the long cardboard mouthpiece. This was very unusual and we were suspicious. Our Yugoslavian translated back and forth. We had a lot of questions. He said we were good workers. What we moved at night kept the production going. In answer to our questions he was realistic and, I believe, honest.

"When will we go home?"

He said German prisoners were generally good workers, and we had to build up what we had destroyed during the war. Russia had lost millions of people in the war and its facilities were pretty much ruined. He gave no dates, no hope for an early return home. We complained about the food, and he told us:

"It will get better. The supply will improve."

He asked us what we got to eat in the camp. He laughed when we told him.

"Russians eat the same. Whatever is shipped into Saratov is shared by all, Russians and Germans."

We were sure Russians had more variety and more quantity. When we asked where the boards go from the mill, he acted as if he did not know. His visit was stimulating! He had made the effort to visit us at two o'clock in the morning to see what these *vojeno plenys* were like. He passed around more *papirosi*, said goodbye, and left. We never saw him again.

My partner and I talked much about the past and our hopes for the future. I was content and healthy. The smell of fresh cut boards created a desire to work with lumber when I got home. Who would need a photographer after the war or someone to direct movies? I could imagine becoming a carpenter and working with my hands.

Our working brigades at the many different plants and factories brought outside news. We got a glimpse of the Russian system and their production methods. Some worked in the tank factory that ran at full capacity. Wasn't the war over? The Russians looked at us *vojeno plenys* with mixed emotions. We were a welcomed workforce, but we reminded them of the war and the suffering they had endured.

Homestead Because we worked at night, we saw more of the activity performed in the camp during the day. We were free and it felt good. Once in a while a guard came by:

"*Davai, chisty!*"

Cleaning. It was more of a symbolic act. No tools, no bucket, no rags, no mops — just a homemade "broom" made from dried branches. We did not disturb too much in our sweeping.

On those warm summer days, I often took a cold shower and dried in the sun. I washed my shirt and underpants. Being in the camp during the day sure had its advantages. Every six to eight weeks when we were deloused they gave us a change of laundry. It was good to wash out my clothes in between.

I had arranged a bunk in the upper room and would sit for a long time on the stairs looking out over the Volga. I forgot everything around me. Hermann Hesse's *Siddhartha* came into my thoughts during those times. When *Siddhartha* came to the ferryman, he spent time learning to listen to the river. Dreams came with the flowing of the water that I could see in the distance. I saw my past — a full, interesting life. What I had done, I did with the fullness of my heart. It was all enjoyment. I saw my little family, my wife Annemarie and son Hans. He was three when I last saw him, now almost a year ago. How old will he be when I come home?

What a beautiful life I had led! With a love for the mountains, I went to Switzerland for the first time when I was just five years old, and again at ages seven and nine. When I was fourteen years old I traveled on my own all around that beautiful country. I recalled those unforgettable scenes before my eyes. When I was sixteen I traveled to Sweden, by ship to Stockholm, and by train to Oslo and Copenhagen, and back to Berlin. I was three days late and school had already started. The trip had been worth the little punishment I received.

Growing up, I always had friends. When Hitler came into power, however, we had conflicts. I was opposed to Hitler and his party from the very beginning. Many of my friends were attracted to the new system. I lost contact with them when I went to Munich to study photography. I wanted to become a movie director. That was my dream, my goal. When a person sits in a darkened theater, the picture is his first impression, then comes the sound or silence to dramatize the picture, and last of all, the dialogue. I feel there is too much talking in movies.

In May 1939, right after my last trip as ship's photographer to New York, Herbert Bode hired me as camera assistant. We had to film the arrival of the

"Legion Condor" in the harbor of Hamburg, and later the troops when they paraded through the Brandenburg Gate in Berlin. This war "exercise" brought Franco into power in Spain, and was a welcome maneuver for Hitler to try out his newly created *Wehrmacht*.

I worked in many films as second assistant. It was a good beginning in the business, until September 1939, when Hitler started the war against Poland.

Soon I was drafted. My home was always where "I hung my hat." Wherever that spot might be, it was home, just as this spot on the stairs was home to me now. The river flowing calmly by represented my past and my future. I didn't try to explain this to anyone. They would not understand the deep peace I had. I knew I would be going to my real home someday. It was just a question of surviving until then.

Franz Franz Gielen, one of our original three, worked only a short time. He had diarrhea from day one at our camp. The long spell when we ate nothing but dry bread did not help. His system would not digest anything anymore. Whatever he ate turned to "water," and came out that way. He got weaker and weaker. The water soups with a drop of oil, cabbage leaves, or green tomatoes made things worse. The small portion of *kasha* or the piece of bread was not the proper food for a person in this condition. Franz was seriously sick.

One day a delegation came into the camp. They were mostly women, all in uniform. They set up quarters in the infirmary.

Günther informed me they wanted to examine everyone in the camp. I asked him how they were set up and he grinned, "You will see."

Since he was "our doctor," he organized the whole procedure. I didn't want to be the first one in, so I got in line with the kitchen staff. We had to take off our shirts to show our upper bodies. I stood before the commissioners who sat in a half circle. I gave my name and was told to drop my pants. I stood there half naked, holding onto my pants with one hand. One of the women doctors made a gesture for me to turn around so they could have a full view of my buttocks.

"*Khorosho.*" (Okay, good.)

I pulled up my pants and went back outside, glad that it was over.

Günther knew I was assigned to Group III. They judged our physical condition by the shape of our rear end. Those who were well formed and solid were Group I, the strongest men, good for any kind of work. Those whose buttocks were not quite as solid but still well formed and otherwise in good shape were in Group II, good for all kinds of work except really heavy labor. Then the ones whose rear was not well formed anymore were assigned to Group III, good for light work only. Who was the judge of what is light and what is heavy work? If we were assigned a job, we were bound to do it first and complain later. Who would listen anyway?

There was even a fourth group called "dystrophy." There was nothing left of their rears and their overall appearance was weak, with no physical strength. Franz Gielen was in the "D" group. No sense keeping them if they can't work anymore. Dead wood. Get rid of them. Send them home? Franz was put on that list.

Those who would be going home were instructed to take nothing except their uniforms and a spoon. No papers, messages, or addresses. Franz's hometown was Berlin. I told him over and over again, and he repeated back to me, the name and address of my mother-in-law — the only one left in Berlin from our family. This was my first chance to send a message home telling them I was alive, where I was, and all of the circumstances. Annemarie and Hans were in Thuringia, and my mother was in Saalfeld. The territory was occupied by Americans at first, and later by the Russians. We did not know if mail would get through, and traveling might be impossible. The best plan was to have Franz go to my mother-in-law.

Every time Franz and I met he repeated the name and address to me. I had confidence he would not forget. Finally the day came when the first transport would leave. Franz and I said good-bye. Tears were in our eyes and we were not ashamed. He thanked me for all I had done for him. It wasn't much, but our relationship had developed into a solid friendship. I wished him God's speed for a safe return to Berlin and watched him march out the gate. It was a relief for all of us left behind to have the really sick prisoners sent home to be taken care of.

Rudi Rudi Strohbach was the only one left of the old crowd back in Stahnsdorf. He was not in the best condition either, but still assigned to Group III. He had a dream that sustained him: to open a restaurant with food from different nationalities and regions in Germany when he got home. He collected recipes from everyone and neatly wrote them down. He was hungry just like everybody else, but "nourished" himself on those recipes. I overheard his conversation with someone about a recipe for a cake his mother had baked; so much flour, sugar and butter, and three eggs. Rudi said:

"Three eggs. I will make it with six or more. That cake will be something special."

Why not? I thought. We didn't have even one egg; six in the cake would be great. Rudi lived on those recipes!

The Yeast Plant

A New Job Our night job at the mill was suddenly shut down. With no assignment, I began to investigate other job possibilities. The Russians had four factories nearby: the sawmill, a distillate, a yeast factory, and a tannery. A couple of them were connected in their production cycle. I had heard good reports about the working condition in the yeast factory. Since I was not assigned to a certain work brigade, I began loitering around the main gate as the brigades went out. I watched closely until the yeast factory was called. Someone was missing. I was close by the gate, available. Before I was able to analyze the situation, I was ordered to join the brigade. Out the gate I went.

It was fall and days and nights were cooler. Most of the jobs in the yeast plant were inside and not just routine. There were all kinds of assignments. But our main job was to help women workers clean and reassemble machinery. Or we worked in the supply rooms, a separate building close to the furnace plant. We helped with loading and unloading supplies, or pumped oil to fill the tanks of the oil burners in the furnace plant when the electric pump refused to work. Our work was always a challenge and fairly interesting. I enjoyed it.

Davai Brigadier Every work brigade had a brigadier in charge. He was responsible to see that all the men were at the gate in the morning, on time, and ready to walk out when the civilian guard came to pick us up. Our guard was a woman, maybe in her early thirties, who came the first week with a gun over her shoulder. I figured she didn't know how to handle it, but it gave her a feeling of authority. One day she did not wear the gun and didn't have it when she returned us to the gate. We never saw the gun again.

Had she sold it? Maybe.

One morning our brigadier was not at the gate. Nobody was in charge. Since I stood closest to him, the Russian guard pointed to me:

"*Davai*, Brigadier." (Go on, you are the brigadier.)

The interpreter grabbed another man from those by the gate to make up the full number. I was the brigadier.

I worked just like everybody else in the yeast plant. But if the foreman wanted something special, she came to me to arrange it. My main responsibility was to see that everybody was ready to go to work in the morning and at the gate at noon for lunch break, as well as at 5:00 P.M., our quitting time. It was only a five-minute walk from the camp.

On the Road My most desirable job was to be on a trip. We never knew what was coming up. There were three of us. We went through the city of Saratov, sometimes out in the countryside. I had the impression most of our trips were illegal. We stole sand, called *tsap-tsarap*, from a construction site or loaded big rocks from some kind of a quarry — always in a hurry. Other times we drove around all day and found nothing. Somehow the "deal" had not worked out. Sitting beside the truck driver was our woman guard without the gun. We called her Magda. She was not a *galina* (pretty young girl). Her round face was expressionless. Did she smile? If ever, it was odd and turned into a grin instead of a joyful expression as a response. Everything visible was round on her. As the face was round, so the two cheeks. Her little black eyes appeared like small holes on both sides of her round nose, which had a reddish shine on its tip. The well-worn and torn *bufaika* (long ski parka) covered everything round underneath, which we could not judge too well since we never saw her without that cover. Her feet were stuck in a pair of oversized felt boots, which gave her an awkward motion in walking — or was that her natural way of moving?

Often Magda wanted us to load up some crummy boards, then sit on them when we passed the guard at the gate of the factory. In that way, she got them outside. We would stop at an open market, where people sell and buy all kinds of things, throw the boards on the ground, and Magda would offer them for sale. People walked by, looked, asked the price, and usually walked away. Magda would get nervous. It was taking too long. Eventually someone came, argued about the price, and finally the boards sold. We drove on and stopped not too far away; Magda mingled in the crowd at the bazaar. She came back with a piece of bread, two fish, and a glass jar with a little vodka. She and the driver had a prassnik (a special celebration) right in the cab. If we were lucky they tossed us a package of makhorka, the rough-cut stems of tobacco plants. When we were extra lucky, they gave us a section of newspaper to make a cigarette.

"*Davai zakurim.*" (Let's have a smoke.)

If a Russian invited us, he would get out a piece of newspaper and give it to us. We would politely tear off a piece of paper and return the rest. He would then reach into another pocket for the *makhorka* and give us just the right amount for a smoke. We spread it carefully in the middle of the paper, rolled it, and licked the long side. We twisted the ends so the precious *tabak* could not fall out. If the mouth end was too tight, we bit it off and lit the cigarette. Surprisingly, the paper did not burn with an open flame. It glowed brightly, but only with a Russian newspaper.

The Yeast Plant

Vodka The storekeeper limped a little, so we called him Humpel. One morning he waited for us at the gate of the yeast plant. I didn't understand a word he said, but talking with his hands and feet, I finally got the picture. He wanted a railroad car moved so it could be unloaded. During the night a boxcar had come in, and the switcher did not push it far enough into the yard of the factory for it to be unloaded. I took the whole brigade down to the boxcar, and with a *lomb* (a big crowbar) and *raz dva vzyali* (one, two, together), the car rolled. When that monster got going, watch out! Fortunately, a brake shoe was in place, and the car stopped right at the ramp for easy unloading. The storekeeper was happy. Humpel told me to come before quitting time and have a drink with him. He snapped his index finger from the thumb to the throat, which meant hard stuff.

As the day went on I forgot all about it. Just before quitting time I made my rounds to get the men together. Humpel saw me and yelled from his storage building, "*Davai, Khansarmin, davai.*"

There is no "h" in the Russian alphabet, so they pronounce the "h" as "kh," as in "ach." So my name was Khansarmin.

Humpel was so glad I had helped him get the railroad car into the right place. He gave me two glass jars. One was filled with pure alcohol — vodka. The other jar was water. I did not know how to drink it. Should I mix it or what? He saw my hesitation and indicated I should take the *schnaps* first, then flush it down with water. I took a sip of the vodka. It burned all the way down! I coughed and reached quickly for the water. Humpel found this funny — me choking on that first swallow. He laughed and laughed. I took a second sip. I had the water jar ready to flush it down immediately. It was somewhat better. I took a third full swallow — the last one — and it almost tasted good. Humpel thought it was the greatest. He slapped me friendly-like on my shoulder.

"*Khorosho, khorosho.*"

I wondered if he meant that for us helping with the railroad car or that I was brave enough to drink that stuff.

I hurried back to the gate. It was an uphill walk, not steep, about four hundred yards. The world suddenly looked different. I walked to the camp on cloud nine. I had a big smile for everyone. When I saw Günther later that evening, he asked:

"Hansarmin, what is the matter with you? Your eyes are so glossy."

In telling him I laughed more than I wanted to. Everything seemed so funny. I slept really well that night. In the days ahead we would often laugh about it as he described very dramatically how I looked and acted.

The Hungarians During the summer months, more and more German prisoners came into our camp. It was refreshing to hear their stories. There were some who fought through Bohemia and pulled back into Bavaria, the southern part of Germany. Some escaped the Russians, who pushed hard from the east, and were captured by the Americans to the west. There must have been thousands or tens of thousands. One day they were ordered onto trucks going east. The war had been over for weeks. Along the road, they met a caravan of Russian trucks, stopped, switched trucks and continued to travel east through Breslau, the common route ending up in Saratov at our camp.

Others told us they were taken captive south of Berlin around the end of April. They tried to get out of a Russian enclosure and fought to the last with tanks and artillery. That could have been the artillery fire we had heard on our march to Sagan.

With their arrival came also a group of about forty *Magyars* (Hungarians). They had fought on our side. Among them was a Hungarian doctor, a full M.D., from Budapest. Through Günther, who was in charge of the sick prisoners, I met the Hungarian doctor. He spoke fluent German. Our relationship grew and we spent many hours together telling stories and exchanging thoughts.

Most of the Hungarian prisoners did not speak German. They knew about as many German words as we knew Russian. A conversation between a Hungarian and a German sounded strange—some words in German, some in Russian, and sometimes the Hungarians acted out what they were trying to say. There were no hard feelings between us. We were all in the same boat, with the hope of going home someday.

Just to be different and to pass the time, I grew a mustache—a handsome handlebar mustache! It gave me something to do, and I needed only my fingers and a little saliva to keep the ends sticking straight out.

Borscht The days grew shorter as it got later in the fall. Silvertooth, one of the factory bosses of the yeast plant, needed three men for a trip. He selected two others and me. One was a little husky fellow, Harold—a happy, easy-going fellow, always with a smile. It was a pleasure to work with him—never complaining. The other one was Karl, a taller guy with a red face and reddish blonde hair. He was a little older than me. Karl had been a small farmer back home. He worried a lot about what might happen to his land and machinery before he could get home.

Silvertooth had a steel upper tooth. He smiled a lot, proudly showing it off. He even smiled when he was angry, which wasn't often. To our surprise, we had to walk on this trip. Silvertooth told us we would be going to his home to cut firewood, and his wife would cook a good *borscht* for us. I remembered it from a small Russian restaurant in Berlin, a delicious soup that they put everything in: cabbage, carrots, red beets, potatoes, pork, beef, spices, and they topped it with sour cream. If it was only half as good as I remembered, it would be a delightful meal. We walked about fifteen minutes to his home, where his wife welcomed us wholeheartedly, pointing to a big pot on the stove that would be our reward. Silvertooth showed us the pile of logs behind the house and brought us the necessary tools to start the job.

We had to fix the sawhorse to make it stable, then tighten the ax handle and sharpen the ax and the two-man handsaw. Silvertooth was pretty well equipped, probably as a result of being the boss of a fairly good-sized plant. He was impressed with the way we prepared the tools. Karl and Harry knew how to cut and split wood, and they taught me. Soon we had a system going. I quickly learned the rhythm needed to pull-push the two-man handsaw so it would not bind. It was all new to me, a city lad. I learned to take a quick look at the piece to be split. If it had a crack, I split it with the ax in the same direction, making it much easier. We took turns working with the saw and the ax and rolled right along. Silvertooth was all smiles. He let his tooth reflect the sunlight, causing it to look like silver. Silvertooth furnished us with *makhorka* and newspaper on our one smoke break. We worked the rest of the day, anxiously looking forward to the soup. We stacked the last piece, cleaned up, and were invited to sit at the dining table where Silvertooth's wife served us the delicious *borscht*. It was worth all our effort!

The house was simple, but neat and clean. The kitchen was a corner of the living room. The well-kept wood floor was not waxed, but spotless. The cupboard and chairs were simple, solidly built, and painted in a faint blue color. Russians seemed to use only two colors: red for the outside and blue for the furniture. The windows were small, but with the early afternoon sunshine streaming through, it was cozy. The stove in the kitchen was also the heating system for the house. I guessed that was the reason there was a stove outside in the yard, to use in the summertime so the cooking would not heat the house — a simple system of air conditioning.

Night Shift

"Chisty, Chisty" When the yeast plant reached full production, a night shift was added from 6:00 P.M. to 6:00 A.M. The yeast plant was typical of other Russian factories with a kitchen and dining room serving at least the lunch meal.

Silvertooth wanted to have Karl, Harold, and me on the night shift. At midnight we were to get meal leftovers from the factory kitchen. He knew we would work and do it right. Or, maybe he thought we could use that extra meal at night. It was such a big deal to allow prisoners outside the camp all night long. Someone finally gave us a blessing, and we had the job. Every night at 6:00 P.M. sharp we were picked up and walked to the plant.

The workers on the night shift were strangers to us, but soon we got to know each other. We were the only men in the production process. The boss of the shift was a pleasant, energetic woman in her early thirties. She was used to giving orders, short and to the point. It was her responsibility to see that shifts produced their quota and more. The work on the night shift was almost pleasant. As we got acquainted we became a part of the team. Mostly we did the heavy work — heavy for the women but not for us — and often the dirtier work. Since the three of us worked all over the plant, there were times when we did not see each other until the midnight break. Our boss, *Natchalnik*, brought us the leftovers from the kitchen. Sometimes it was warmed up, sometimes it was cold, but it was an additional meal for us. The woman saw to it that we had a table and chairs where we could enjoy our dinner. Most of the workers had to eat right at their working places.

One of my jobs was to clean the huge, two-story-high storage tanks. The brew that eventually became yeast left its marks and some suds. The tanks had to be washed and cleaned thoroughly. I must have done the job right because they looked for me whenever that cleaning job came up. The women never remembered my name. They asked:

"Where is...?" imitating me twirling my handlebar mustache. I needed rubber boots and a rubber apron to do the job, and soon worked out a routine to wash the tank without getting wet. I took my time and did a good job. No hurry! No *davai*! The warm water from the hose created damp, warm air — almost tropical. Maybe nobody else wanted to do that job. This procedure came up twice during each shift. I liked it.

My other job was with a couple of centrifuges. After each process the machines had to be taken apart and cleaned. The centrifuges were quite large. A small crane was mounted on the ceiling to assist in the process of moving the parts to be cleaned to a basin about the size of a bathtub. The woman who worked with those centrifuges had quite a job. She was a little on the heavy side, not too tall, with a round face and reddish blonde hair combed straight back and held in a tight knot. She was always in a good mood. She smiled as she instructed me about how to take apart the machines. If I ever had a problem, she gladly helped. She always worked by herself and was pleased to have my company.

One night she was more smiles than usual. In my limited Russian, I got the picture. Her husband had finally come home. I had detected long before that she was lonely and missed her husband. That night, when I came in to check for the service of centrifuges, I could not believe my eyes. She was in the tub taking a bath. She laughed at me when I looked stunned. She sang, and I heard:

"*Chisty, chisty.*" (Clean, clean.)

That husband had a clean wife that night.

Postcard As we woke up from our day sleep to get our lunch soup, something was in the air. We could feel it. Word spread around in a hurry. Each prisoner would receive one blank postcard from the Russian Half Moon, an organization similar to the International Red Cross. Finally, we could write home!

It was a double card. On one card we wrote the address in German and a message on the back. The attached card had to be addressed in Cyrillic lettering for it to be returned to us from our loved ones. I did not know the Russian alphabet well enough, so Günther wrote my name and return address. Only those who received a card from a prisoner were able to write in return. Yes, "*mail budit*" was promised in June and fulfilled at the end of November 1945. It was a great morale boost. All kinds of thoughts came into my mind. To whom should I write the first card? What could I say to indicate my well-being without revealing anything that might not be passed by Russian mail censors? We were told not to write the location of the camp and the kind of work we did. I decided to write this first card to my mother-in-law in Berlin. Mail would go faster to the capital than to the countryside in Thuringia, where Annemarie and my mother lived. She would be able to pass the news to them.

The same night I took my postcard to the plant. I knew there was ink in the laboratory. During break I asked the chemical engineer in charge if I could write the first card home using his ink.

"Yes, come, sit at my table."

He brought pen and ink from his desk, and I wrote the first message home. The words went through my mind so many times. I had been a prisoner for seven months — the things that had happened in all that time! I filled the entire space with questions about my loved ones at home and letting them know that I was all right and in good health.

The rumors about the war's end were difficult to understand. We heard Germany had been divided into occupation territories and Berlin had some special arrangements. Had Franz Gielen made it to Berlin and remembered the address of my mother-in-law?

Christmas Cookies As Christmas drew near, Günther and I made plans to bake cookies. I brought yeast from the yeast plant. He got flour from the bakery brigade. The guys were husky and worked hard, moving flour sacks from trucks to storage and from storage to the top of the dough machines. The flour sacks were not so bad. They were heavy but fit around the shoulder and back. But the bags of salt, coarse like rocks, were sometimes painful. This was our elite brigade. Not only could they eat all the bread they wanted, they could also take a shower every day before they came home. One man succeeded in getting into that brigade, but gave up after one day. It was hard work. A person had to be built for it. I was satisfied with my job in the yeast plant.

Günther and I both saved the little butter and sugar we sometimes got for our cookies. Nobody but the guys working in the kitchen knew how much really went into the food and how much disappeared before it got into the kettle. The butter ration was one level teaspoon, and the sugar ration was a level tablespoon or less. Those portions were given to us in our open hand. We had to plan in advance how to dispose of the butter or sugar: Some put it in a little sack to eat at another time; some put it on a slice of bread just received; others passed it on to another buddy in exchange for tobacco; some dumped the sugar and/or butter into the soup; others right into their mouths with no fuss, no mess — why bother? It was gone. I brought my little bit of butter to Günther. He kept it safe in his upstairs room, which was impossible in the mass quarters I lived in. I had made a small bag from an old shirt for the sugar rations. Günther and I wanted to do something special for some close buddies as a Christmas surprise. Fortunately this camp was blessed with plenty of firewood from the mill.

One evening Günther and I carried all our saved ingredients into the doctor's office and started preparing the dough. As we remembered from days long past, we set the yeast with warm water and some flour as Mother had done back home for a yeast cake. In the meantime we mixed the rest of the flour with the sugar, then added water and the precious little bit of butter we had saved. We talked in whispers so the patients in the bedroom next door would not hear us. We waited for about an hour, but the yeast did not rise. Finally, we had to finish our task and put everything together. Now we rolled the dough with our bare hands, formed the cookies, and placed them on the hot metal sheet of the little heating stove. They turned a light brown color and smelled so good — real, homemade cookies. It was like home when Mother did the Christmas baking. Günther hid them in a safe place in the infirmary. It was late when I got into my bunk. We had eaten only one cookie each, just to taste them, and were they delicious! We were as happy as little kids to think about surprising our buddies on Christmas Eve.

My last thought before going to sleep was: We had beaten this rotten system. What a lift, doing something out of the ordinary! The joy of planning and preparing those cookies and the thought of sharing them on Christmas put me into a peaceful sleep.

The next morning we did not have to go to work. We had Saturdays and Sundays off since we worked Monday night through Friday night — twelve-hour shifts. I was one of the last to go down for morning soup and the single piece of bread. We three had to go together since we were counted as a brigade.

As I passed the infirmary, Günther waved at me and said, "The cookies are gone!"

That was a blow almost as bad as having been taken prisoner, something you expected toward the end of war and a relief to have it over. But losing those cookies — an incredible disappointment!

"Are you sure?"

Looking bewildered, he said, "I know where I hid them last night. The cloth we wrapped them in is still there — empty."

We reconstructed what might have happened. Perhaps the patients in the infirmary smelled something baking that night. They had only to follow their noses right to our hiding place. We never found out for sure what happened. It was not legal to bake the cookies, and it was certainly not fair for someone else to search them out and eat them. I guess one wrong cancelled out the other.

Chai Back on the night shift, the woman who had taken a bath in the parts cleaning tub was happier than I had ever seen her. She was radiant. Finally I had a name for her — Joy.

That night I inquired how it was best to bake with the yeast. She laughed, like it was a dumb question.

"This is not baking yeast. It is a medical supplement yeast added to meals."

Here was the reason our dough would not rise, but also it would not hurt the patients who had eaten the cookies.

On one of our night breaks, either the kitchen forgot to send something for us three *vojeno plenys* or there was nothing left over. The head woman of the night shift assured us we would have something to eat and *chai* (tea) *budit* it would be. I remarked to Karl and Harold: "Boy, we get Russian tea. That is a treat!"

I remembered long before the war when I was invited for an afternoon snack and was served Russian tea. It was dark and strong and delicious.

That dear woman also brought us some boiled potatoes, salt, and pieces of bread like we had in camp.

"*Chai budit.*"

The tea would come right away. The potatoes, bread, and salt came from the girls on the night shift. They had shared so we could have something to eat. This act showed best the relationship that those women had with us. We were their equals and on a human level — nothing divided us from each other. Our forewoman came in with a big, steaming pot.

"*Chai yest.*" (It is tea.)

I lifted the lid, prepared to enjoy the aroma of fresh-brewed Russian tea. There was no aroma. All that was in the pot was hot water. I called her back.

"*Chai nyet.*" (No tea.)

She turned around and pointed to the pot of water.

"It is tea."

Later I found out that during and after the war, hot water was called tea (with or without leaves). There had been sacrifices on all sides through this war.

Does happiness depend on tea leaves? I asked myself.

Be glad to have hot water to drink.

With My Bare Hands Late one night I was ordered to go to the heating plant next to the warehouse. The mechanic was waiting for me impatiently. He explained briefly that it was an emergency. I should climb a ladder to a small platform and swing the handle of the oil pump, which was automatically oiled by the process of pumping oil into the tank. It was pleasantly warm in the heating plant, so I took off my coat as I pumped. A call came from below. The tank was full, the oil overflowing. I was allowed to come down from my high platform. Since I had worked very fast, there was no need to pump for several hours. The engineer indicated that I could sleep by holding his hands together and laying his head on them. That was the right job. I was willing to come back anytime.

As I looked around, he explained the system to me. Inside the firehold the heating oil would run into a shallow pan and be sprinkled with water, which would run over the burning oil. He claimed it created a more intensive flame and more heat. It seemed to work well. The heating plant provided the hot water and heat for all of the surrounding buildings.

I bedded down on the dirt floor with my overcoat as a mattress and felt warm as the roaring noise of the furnace filled the room. I fell asleep. I was awakened by something crawling under my jacket. I grabbed it. Here I was half awake with a mouse in my hand underneath my shirt. It struggled, and as I squeezed tighter, it gave up. It was an odd sensation. I reached in with my other hand and pulled it out from under my shirt. That was the first and last time that I caught a mouse with my bare hands — asleep or awake. After that experience, I wasn't tired anymore.

With nothing to do, too warm and too uncomfortable to sleep, I became bored. But I knew I had to operate that pump one more time. Fortunately my forewoman came. She argued with the engineer and won. I was glad to be out at last. What I had thought an "opportunity" never came again.

Night Shift

A Fill-In During our free time between shifts we cleaned the barracks (once in a while), cleaned the latrine (on the surface), slept, and were careful not to miss the meal between shifts. Occasionally a job came up outside camp, but never anything exciting.

Once two of us volunteered for one of those jobs. Harold, the stout one with the smiling face, and I were sent after produce. Produce sounded like something to eat. If nothing else, we would be out of the camp for a while and on the road to someplace.

After we had loaded some empty barrels from the magazine, Harold and I jumped on the rear of the truck and it took off. Most of those trucks were at least two tons and rode like tanks. When empty, they were even worse. We hung on for dear life. The springs must have been steel bars. We felt every bump and every hole in the road, but learned to stay flexible in our knees to absorb the jolts. Through the rear window of the cab we saw the driver and the civilian in the front jostling around and laughing. They were having a great time. We drove far outside the city into nowhere: a hilly countryside with hardly any trees, open fields as far as one could see — neither plowed nor attended — just lying there. We stopped by a single big tree that must have been a landmark or orientation point. The earth was mounded over some type of underground structure. The civilian unlocked the door. I was standing next to him and curious about what might be inside. He pointed to a pair of rubber boots, a shovel, and some buckets. It seemed to be a storage facility for *capusta* (sauerkraut). The temperature inside was pleasantly cool, but a penetrating smell came from the sauerkraut. I wondered how long it had been stored. I stepped into the storage pit with boots on and took on the kraut swamp. The bucket I filled sank in a bit. My boots kept getting stuck, and I almost pulled out a bare foot now and then. But I learned to walk as I filled the buckets. Harold carried them to the truck, and the civilian dumped them into the barrels.

The cabbage is layered with salt in between and stored for a long time as it turns sour. Since we had six buckets but only two and one-half guys working (the half was the civilian who dumped the kraut into the barrels), I suddenly realized I was filling the buckets too fast — faster than Harold could carry them to the truck. I slowed down. If we had to fill all the barrels on the truck, it would take forever. I noticed the driver, who was doing nothing, was getting nervous, looking at his watch, and shouting:

"*Davai, bistro.*" (Faster, faster.)

I stopped working and shouted back at him:

"*Nyet khorosho.*" (It is not good.)

If he would help, we could fill all six buckets and there would be no delay. The driver cursed me: "Jump on your mother."

But he pitched in and helped us, and we got a good production line going. Harold had the hardest job, but he didn't seem to mind. He always had a smile, and that even rubbed off on the driver. Harold started to hum and finally to sing, giving rhythm to the bucket brigade. I had to work faster to keep up. I dug the kraut soft spots to fill the buckets without so much effort. The hard spots stood rigid, upright. I kicked at them, and they broke up and were easier to dig. All the barrels were completely filled except one that was only two-thirds full. Finally we were finished.

The civilian shut the door:

"*Khorosho.*"

I gestured that only with their help had it been done. We two *vojeno plenys* could not have made it alone. They laughed. Did they think we had tricked them into helping us, or were they just happy because the work was done in good time?

The ride back to the camp was a little smoother with the load on the truck. Harold and I ate some of the most tender cabbage leaves. We felt it was a just reward for our labor.

The driver took a different road back. At the outskirts of Saratov we stopped at a house.

"*Davai, davai.*"

The four of us quickly unloaded the barrel filled only two-thirds and carried it behind the house. The driver went inside, came out after a while, and we headed for the camp.

When we arrived at the gate the bakery brigade was ready to go inside. These were our strongest men, and our guard got them to unload the full barrels. For them it was nothing. And were Harold and I relieved! We both smelled like sauerkraut when we got back to our quarters.

The Bath Our work in the yeast plant became an even trot. We knew what had to be done and when. We moved around freely and began to get ideas. It was as if we were at home. Encouraged by Joy, the bathing lady, I watched operations closer and noticed that during break time nobody went into the room with the centrifuges. On one break, I filled the cleaning tub with hot water, undressed, and jumped in. What an experience — my whole body surrounded by warm water! I know how Joy felt when she had taken her bath to meet her husband. I wished for some soap, but rubbing my skin produced a sensational feeling. I did not spend much time in the tub since I had no towel to dry myself with. My shirt was a good substitute, and within minutes I was dressed again and watching the water gurgle out of the tub. No evidence. How clean I felt! I hung my shirt over a steam pipe to dry. When I picked it up later, my dried "towel shirt" had a broad, almost black-grey stripe across it. That steam pipe had collected dirt over the years. The next night I washed that "clothesline pipe" until it was cleaner than it had ever been before. Every now and then I took my secret bath and felt no guilt. I enjoyed this pleasure for quite some time, until one night, just as I got out of my "bathtub" and started to dry off, the door opened and the woman foreman came in, stopped, and shouted:

"*Nix cultura.*"

She ran out and slammed the door. That was the end of my bathing. She never said anything to me, and I did not mention it either. But somehow the trust was broken. Not too long afterwards, our night shift came to an end. Was it because of my bathing? We had had it too good for a long time.

In Between Jobs

The Honey Wagon Was it a coincidence that the two events happened simultaneously, or was I just in the wrong place at the wrong time, or did our interpreter, who was in a way in charge of the camp, know about the bath incident? I never found out, but it did not change the situation.

About every two months, the honey wagon came into camp to clean the latrine. The operator was a little old man who wore the same half-torn fur coat and fur cap summer and winter. He never smiled, never argued, never showed any emotion at all. He just did what he was told to do. The little horse that pulled the honey wagon seemed as old as its driver. It was a miniature kind of covered wagon without a cover. Between the rungs on both sides was the great barrel with an opening on the top to load, and at the rear an opening to empty the contents. I happened to be too close when the driver came in with his honey wagon, and I was ordered to spoon the latrine. You did this by pouring the bucket mounted at the end of a long wooden handle into the barrel. The trick was to hit the opening at the top without spilling the contents. I did my best. Guys who had done it before asked me if this was my first time.

"Yes," I replied.

They advised me to be careful unloading, and to stay as far as possible to the side of the wagon when opening the gate so as not to get it all over myself. They spoke from experience, I assumed.

I trembled after I had it all loaded. The little old driver and I went out of the camp to a nearby field to unload. Should I be on the left or the right side of the wagon? I had forgotten to ask, and they had only said: "Stay away as far as you can."

I decided to stay on the left side and pull the handle with my right hand — right to left and jump. The old man gave me the sign to open the gate. The wagon kept going. I tried to stop it. He lifted his arm again, signaling that I should open the gate. My heart was in my hand as I gave the handle a quick jerk. It opened very easily. I ran toward the driver. There was a second's delay before the contents gushed out. That second saved me! The contents emptied by gravity as the driver edged uphill. He stopped and I closed the gate. It was over. My heart was pounding. I was concentrating on doing it right and avoiding disaster because we could not send out clothes to the cleaners. I was aware that what I did was for the good of all in the camp. I promised myself to carefully instruct anyone else drafted for this duty. The guard at the gate looked me over, took a smell, and then said:

"*Khorosho.*" (Well done, you are lucky.)

One Escapes We had the usual roll call. Every evening we were counted, recounted a second and a third time. It was normal procedure; we were used to it — nothing extraordinary. Some made funny remarks, you could hear laughter here and there. Close to me I heard the remark:

"Three hundred eighty-four all week long. Did somebody sneak into the camp for a weight reduction program with our hot water soups?"

But now we noticed the interpreter and the German commandant running around. The Russian commandant, as he liked to be called, waited for the report of the correct count. Even Günther, our physician, got involved and counted. The interpreter and our German commandant started to search every room, the infirmary, the latrine, kitchen, dining hall, washroom, and every corner of the camp yard.

Usually the count came to an end. "All present," was the report to the commandant. He was happy and we were dismissed.

What was the matter tonight? Even the Russian commandant moved from his stoic position, the spot where every night he received the count report. He walked through the rows counting the men one by one. Remarks became more specific:

"Why didn't you bring your abacus?"

We called it the "idiot's harp." (We were the real idiots because we had not figured out how to use it.)

Finally word spread around: One man was missing. Who could it be? The count was less one! Had someone escaped? Who had the guts to try? Would he know Russian well enough to get through? How far was it to the German border? We had never seen a map. We knew Saratov was located on the Volga, but how far was it from home? One thousand miles? Two thousand miles, more or less? Nobody knew for sure, except that it was a long way home. At least he had picked a good season. It was harvest time in many regions, so he could find something to eat in the fields along the way. The first thought a prisoner has is: 'Where will I find food?' Whoever he was, we admired him. He had guts! I wished him well. Let him get through.

The search continued. Our interpreter turned more pale than usual. He was nervous, like it was his fault someone had escaped. Eventually somebody had the bright idea to divide us into our working brigades to see who the missing one was. The brigadier of each brigade knew his men and would know quickly who was missing. The brigadiers raised their hands and shouted the name of their brigade to assemble on his spot. It did not take long. Every brigadier counted his men. Lo and behold, from the sawmill brigade one man was missing. It had turned dark in the meantime.

"One man missing!"

All were happy, except the Russian commandant.

He was mad. He would have to write a report to some higher office. Would he get some bad marks? The word came in short sentences. The interpreter translated for us, and we looked very serious and nodded our heads.

First, he ordered guards to search the sawmill complex. That could take the poor guys all night — it was a big area. Between wood piles, bushes and high grass, buildings and machinery, there were hundreds of places to hide — if he was not gone by now. The dark protected him well.

The commandant turned to us.

"I will alert the militia in every city, every village — The prisoner will be shot if found — He will be returned to the camp, dead or alive — Our system catches any fugitive — He will not get very far."

And on and on.

"There are border guards — No one can get out of Russia — And even if a man makes it home, he will be arrested and brought all the way back to this camp, where he belongs."

It took a long time for the commandant to run out of steam. We were finally dismissed. It was long past bedtime.

Someone eased the pressure with the remark:

"The cook promised we would all get another fingernail full of *kasha* for the noon meal. The portion of the one missing will be distributed equally between all of us."

There was a last laugh, and a good night's sleep was had by all.

The guys from his brigade were surprised. He was a quiet guy, pleasant to work with, never said a word to anyone. He had planned it by himself. And now he was on his way. Good luck old fellow, I hope you make it! Or?

Too Much I helped out here and there on different brigades, but nothing was exciting. We were spoiled by our twelve-hour shifts at the yeast plant and the good relations we had with those night workers. I got excited about a possible opening at the tannery. I knew the sawmill, the yeast plant, and here was a chance to get into the tannery. The spirit plant was pretty much taboo for *vojeno plenys*. They had a brigade of only three men who had been working there a long time. They would not be allowed at the end of the line where the liquor bottles were filled. One of the guys at the spirit plant did manage to drink some. Nobody knew how he did it or how much he had. His two buddies carried him limp through the gate. The guard laughed. The boys carried him to his bunk and there he lay, pale and lifeless. If you drank that concentrated liquor without water, it could kill you. He survived and confessed — never again.

It was early spring of 1946. We talked often about the good times we had had on the night shift at the yeast plant, and how well we had come through the winter. Good things cannot last forever.

Buttocks Show It was buttocks show again, dividing us into rear-end groups. It became routine: walking in without shirts, giving your name, dropping your pants, turning around to show your buttocks, pulling up your pants and walking out. I came out of one of those visits in Group II. I must have gained weight, and it showed in the rear. Maybe that additional midnight meal at the yeast plant added additional pounds.

It had been a blessing to be out of the camp, as well as working with people other than prisoners. We had seen it with our own eyes — the Russians were not much better off than us prisoners. But they had to live under those conditions for the rest of their lives. We hoped to go home someday.

I was content with whatever came each day. I thanked God before each meal and thanked Him afterward for whatever I had received. I always got up filled. I could have eaten more, but I learned to be content in abundance and with little. One day the soup had something solid in it — more potatoes and less *capusta*. As I came out of the dining hall, a guy said to me, "I could have eaten a bucketful of that soup."

I remarked, "If you had that bucketful today, you would get twice as hungry tomorrow. Our stomachs are shrunk and used to getting little at meals. If we overload our stomachs, they will want the same amount tomorrow. And we will feel hungrier the next day. So be content with what you get."

He looked at me, not understanding what I was talking about.

At the last rear-end presentation, I was upgraded, but Rudi Strohbach was downgraded to "D" for dystrophic, which meant no work and a good chance of being sent home. And he was. But it took a long time to gather all the prisoners from different camps and hospitals to make up the transport.

Then "*Davai, davai.*" (Hurry, hurry. Get out of here.) Since Rudi's hometown was also Berlin, I gave him the address of my mother-in-law in Berlin. We did not know if Franz Gielen had made it home, and if he remembered the address and made the visit. Rudi was another hope. When he came to say goodbye, I realized how much weight he had lost. When you see someone every day, it's so gradual you don't notice it. Rudi was full of hope, but in our good-byes there was sadness, too. We had gone through tough times, and tough times bind men together more than anything else. I encouraged him to take the message home to my family that I was alive and well and making the best of every situation. I wondered if Rudi took all the recipes he had collected. They had sustained him up to this time. Now he was the lucky one, going home. He had paid the price — physically weak and not worth being fed anymore.

Downtown I was the only one left in the camp of our original troop. I wondered what happened to all the others.

During an odd assignment, I had the chance to be on transport. Transport had only two meanings for a *vojeno pleny*: either transport home or transport to the hospital. Or, one of the daily assignments — to be transported around on a truck to load or unload whatever it might be. I loved to be on the move, always something new to see, never knowing where it might lead to, always adjusting to new situations, from honest pickup and delivery to hurry-up loading of a *tsap-tsarap* and blatant stealing. On those trips a civilian was usually with us on the truck. Those guards seemed proud to be seen with a rifle over their shoulder. Either one of two things seemed to lift a person out of ordinary civilian status: carrying a gun and having the authority to watch over somebody, or guarding things that someone might want to steal, such as harvest in a field or items in storage, even in a factory building. But real authority was carrying a briefcase — a nine- by twelve-inch leather case slung over the shoulder by a leather strap or just a string. We had such cases in the German Army to hold maps and writing supplies.

As we entered the town, our guard gestured at everything the eye could see: streets, apartment buildings, streetcars, "all ours." He was impressed with himself and all that belonged to the people. He must have come from some country village. I faced him and said:

"Yes, but what is yours?"

And again, with a big gesture, he pointed at everything around us. I repeated my question and pointed at him personally:

"What is yours — your own?"

He looked at me like I had not understood him, so I pointed like he did.

"Yes, all yours. But what is your personal own?"

He caught on and acted like he would beat me with his rifle butt.

"Capitalist, capitalist!"

I enjoyed the ride through the city. I saw Russians walking the street — men and women carrying shopping bags and baskets, waiting for the "tramway," lined up at a store front to purchase a hard-to-get item. I remembered back home we had to line up to get tickets for special concerts or theater plays. People are people, everywhere — except when ideology gets in the way.

Music of the Spheres The evening meal was finished. I had spooned my soup slowly out of the tin bowl. It had a little taste. What made it more palatable than at other times? I kept my bread to eat for dessert. I had no plans. I just hit the sack. It felt good having the leisure, satisfied with the hot water soup and the slice of bread in my linen bag to eat later. It was not white anymore. With time it had turned into a grayish tone. Like everything around us, gray and more gray. Best not to look around you and start brooding. Pick a joyful thought and dwell on that.

Loudspeakers were in every room, but there was never any sound. Maybe they blasted orders, announcements, and propaganda during the time it was used for Russian civil prisoners. Suddenly a noise came out of those small wooden boxes!

Music? I heard orchestra and piano in harmonious simplicity and grand melodies. Beauty in this dreary place? I was overwhelmed. I closed my eyes. I leaned forward to hear the beautiful music in its fullness. I absorbed every tone. What a change from melancholic routine to triumphant joy! Shivers went down my spine. Memories came. Where had I heard that music the last time? In a concert hall in Munich? Berlin?

Here in a prisoner of war camp, was I allowed to hear it? High and low, fast and slow, forte to pianissimo, tender and rough, orchestra and piano competing with each other, and then harmonizing. I took it all in. Oh, would it come never to an end!

I heard a winter storm and blowing snow, a calm breeze in the sunshine, raindrops and a downpour. It came in sounds to me, what little I had seen and experienced of this great Russian land. With my eyes closed, I saw for the first time the beauty, the contrast, the greatness of this huge, wide land of Russia. This music symbolized Russia to me. I could feel what the people called "Motherland Russia."

May some of these melodies stay with me, that I may recall them anytime I want to. The music came to the closing chords like a big exclamation mark. The Concerto for Piano and Orchestra No. 1 by Pyotr Ilich Tchaikovsky. To me it was a touch of heaven on earth.

A last click of the loudspeaker, then silence. I had to come back. Where was I? In music, in memories, in places I had seen of this country? I was filled with calm, joyful harmony.

Who had turned the switch for this beautiful music to come into our camp? Was it by accident, or did somebody who enjoyed music want us to hear it, too? Whatever the reason, it was the only time that music came from those speakers. The spider inside the speaker box could continue to weave his web, not to be disturbed by sound or vibration.

Half and Half In the monotony of camp life, it was good to do something just to be different. On the spur of the moment, I went to the barber room and asked Erich, our head barber, when I could have my handlebar mustache shaved off. He was surprised, but said for me to sit down. Erich's razors were never too well sharpened. The whistle blew for evening count just as he had shaved the left side. I walked outside and stepped into line. The left side of my mustache was gone, but the right side was still proudly in place. I looked straight ahead. The guy to my left said:

"Hansarmin, what happened to your mustache?"

The guy on the right said:

"What do you mean? He still has his handlebars."

Slowly I turned to the left, and the guys on that side had a good laugh. I turned slowly to the right so they too could see that half of it was gone. More laughter. After the count I had the other half shaved off and decided no more mustache growing. I'd get shaved once in a while like everybody else. For a long time afterward, some of my buddies mourned the loss of my handlebars by twirling imaginary bars on both ends.

Tannery

Another New Job Finally I made a new beginning at the tannery. The guys who had been there a long time had steady assignments. Since I was a newcomer I was shuffled around to jobs nobody wanted to do anymore: carrying hides, cleaning them, and so on. Before I could establish a routine in one job, I was moved to something else. Nothing seemed special or exciting. But in moving around, I learned how the plant operated. I ended up at the pits, to keep moving cowhides in the lye and then from one pit of lye to the next. Large basins were built into the floor. They were filled with different concentrations of lye. The hides had to be moved from one pit to the other until all the hair was gone. A long heavy stick was used to move the hides as carefully as possible in order not to splash lye on ourselves. I watched how the Russians did it. They were experts at the job. I tried it. To my surprise, if I tried to move a hide and did not quite make it, one of the others helped me with his long stick. No one was in a hurry.

Whenever I had a chance, I looked around to see what else there was to do. As the days went by, I got glimpses of the leather process. The plant handled pigskins and cowhides. After the last lye pit, the hides were hairless. They had to be washed thoroughly in order to put them into an oak bath where they remained for several days. This was the actual tanning. Then they went into the drying chamber—the final operation. The tannery got more interesting as I did different jobs.

Talon Budit One morning the *Natchalnik* came for me. I don't know why he chose me, since the others had been there much longer. He took me to one of the smaller pits: about four feet wide, six or seven feet long, and three feet deep. Would I clean it out? He didn't order me, he asked me and said it would get me a *talon* (a ticket for a meal in the factory dining room). A prisoner of war will do anything for an extra meal. I said, "*Da*." Yes, I would do it. The pit was full of black mud. I filled a bucket and carried it outside to dump it. It was awkward carrying just one bucket without spilling it on my pants and shoes. I asked for a second bucket. One in each hand balanced the load and made carrying easier. The Russian in charge looked at me a bit surprised, but pointed to where I could find another one. I filled both buckets, but not quite so full. I developed a system. The carrying was easy and nothing spilled. It's the secret of any kind of labor—find a system and the job will be only half as difficult. The level of the mud in the pit sank slowly. The job reminded me of the *capusta* digging with Harold. The *Natchalnik* was surprised to see how much I had gotten done and promised again, "*Talon budit.*" Did this mean I would get two *talons*? I couldn't finish the work in one day. The next morning I asked the boss for a pair of rubber boots. He looked astonished at my request but brought me a pair and said to return them to him personally. I considered the job a good physical workout. With the boots I could jump into the pit and make it somewhat fun to dig the mud out. Around noon, I was finished. I washed up, cleaned the shovel, boots, and buckets, and returned the rubber boots to the *Natchalnik*. His only comment:

"*Khorosho.*"

I asked him, "*Talon yest?*"

"*Talon budit.*"

He made a gesture that meant he did not have one with him. I hounded him every day, and he began avoiding me. After a few days had passed, I ran into him.

"*Talon yest?*"

Before he could come up with an excuse, I told him in the little Russian I could speak that he was not a good *Natchalnik*. I had done my work. He had promised me a *talon*, and I did not yet have it. He looked surprised and smiled at my words. Had any prisoner of war ever told him off like that before? He raised his hands to calm me down.

"*Talon budit, budit.*"

Later he looked me up and took me to the dining hall. The service counter was already cleaned and the food put away. He talked to the girl in charge and she looked at me as if to say: He is just a prisoner of war! But one of the cooks filled a bowl to the rim with *kasha*, and I sat down to eat. I waved at the *Natchalnik*, smiled and said:

"*Spasibo.*" (Thank you.)

This was more *kasha* than we got in a whole week at the camp, and it was better prepared and tastier. I enjoyed it immensely and ate very slowly. How grateful I was for that extra meal, and I thanked God for his kindness to me. After that experience, I knew one had to stand up to the Russians or else they would not do what they promised.

Russian Prisoners of War As I ate the bowl of *kasha*, I remembered Russian prisoners of war in Berlin. I was assigned to a special unit that had a branch office in Berlin. I had been in a car accident in Estonia, close to Dorpat, and wound up in the University Hospital with a concussion, a broken arm, and a fracture of the upper jaw. I was ordered to stay in Berlin during my convalescence and assist in the Berlin office, located in an apartment on the fourth floor. One day bombs hit this apartment complex and it burned down. Only the walls were left standing. Our unit had aerials stored in the cellar that had to be dug out and secured. I got the order for this assignment. I drove out to the prison camp in Zehlendorf to pick up eight Russian prisoners of war, signed for the men, and marched them down the street to the *S-Bahn*, the commuter train to Berlin. We traveled free with a special permit. Some of the Russians spoke German fairly well, not only to communicate, but well enough for a conversation.

As the men dug, they came upon a destroyed den and found two cigarette tins that were made before the war when cigarettes were sold in packs of fifty and one hundred. The tins would be collectors' items by now, and they were full of German pfennige (pennies). They tried to give the money to me, but I told them they found the treasure and it was theirs. They counted almost eight marks. That broke the ice between us.

I had previously arranged with a small restaurant close by to serve lunch for eight Russian prisoners of war. I knew it would be *markenfrei* (a meal without ration coupons) and we all had a beer with the meal. The beer during the war was lean, with almost no alcohol. We sat at one table in the corner of the restaurant and no one bothered us. In their digging they also came upon a bottle of hair tonic and a bottle of Eau de Cologne. I did not pay any attention to what they did with it. When we went for lunch that day they whispered together, and the leader handed the bottle to me under the table to pour some hair tonic into my beer. I thanked him for the offer, but declined. He asked if they could spike their beers, and they did. "*Prosit* (cheers)." The prisoners had exceptional table manners, pouring their share of the hair tonic into their beer under the table so other guests would not notice. They were treated fairly and were happy.

On the way back to camp, they wanted to stop at a bakery. They had German bread ration coupons traded for the carved children's toys they had made in camp. But prisoners could not go into a bakery and buy bread. They asked if I would do it for them. I did.

Now to the important part: When we came to the camp gate, they knew the German guards might take their bread. They knew how to handle that problem. I should take the bread and tell the guard those prisoners worked so well that a woman gave them the bread, and I wanted to be sure they got it.

"Yes, corporal," the guard said.

Before I left I waited until they went through the gate, and the guard gave them the loaf of bread.

Sure enough, the Russian prisoners dug clear down to the cellar floor, and we found the aerials and secured them. They asked me if I had another job for them to do — anything. We took one more day to fill in the hole they had dug, but after lunch we were finished. They did not want to go back to camp in the early afternoon where they would have to do odd chores. I came up with an idea.

The glass of a balcony door of my mother's apartment in Berlin had been broken during one of the air attacks. We drove into a different part of the city to the apartment on the third floor. They took the door off its hinges and carried it down the stairs to a nearby glass shop. The glazier could glaze it right away. When finished, the gang carried it back and cleaned the broken glass off the floor and rehung it. They did a good job and enjoyed the work.

My mother, who was evacuated to the Thuringia countryside during the war, had a map of Europe on the wall. Perhaps she wanted to be reminded where Waldemar, my brother, was buried. It was a good-sized map with western Russia showing. The Russians were full of enthusiasm when they saw the map. They showed me where the Russian front was located the day before. They had an illegal homemade radio in the camp and were better informed than we Germans.

Here in the apartment, we said our good-byes. Everyone wanted to shake hands with me and stood at some kind of attention. They appreciated the way I had treated them. I took them back to the gate for the last time and passed a loaf of bread through for them "for the good work done." They stood behind the barbed wire and waved at me. I had to act "official," so I saluted the men and turned away without looking back. A shiver went down my spine thinking about what might happen to these decent human beings.

Just a Spoon I finally finished my kasha at the tannery. What a treat it was after cleaning out the pit! I set my empty, really clean bowl on the counter. The spoon just happened to fit perfectly in my upper pocket. I remembered a saying I learned in the early days as a recruit back in 1935: Nothing is ever stolen, it only changes owners. Now I had a replacement for my lost spoon. After standing up to the *Natchalnik*, we had good rapport thereafter. I got jobs with more "freedom" and better flexibility. Whenever there was a need to get something done, I was assigned most often. I did not mind. I ended up in the drying chamber where the finished hides were hung to dry. Those wet cowhides were heavy and I worked by myself. I soon found a way to hang them on the wood beams by pulling the front legs over first and then pulling until the whole hide hung clear. The heaviest part was the rear of the hide.

In the evening at camp we sat around and shared our job experiences. I told some of the guys what I did at the tannery. Nobody thought much about what I said until the next day when one of those guys contacted me. He wanted to know if I could get a piece of leather for the soles of a pair of shoes. Somebody in the factory where he worked would pay a good price for it. I did not promise anything. As I swung around on those beams in the drying chamber, nobody kept up with me. They only knew I did my job. What I needed was a sharp knife. Bruno said he would make one for me since he had access to broken hacksaw blades. He ground one down on one side and put a wooden handle on it.

"That's yours for keeps," he said.

Tannery

What a luxury—a knife in the prison camp! The only problem was there wasn't much to cut. There were woodcarvers in the camp who made all kinds of things: wooden pipes, tobacco boxes, and children's toys. I had heard about those in Berlin-Zehlendorf with the Russian prisoners of war. I could always trade the knife or lease it out. It had value!

Tsap-Tsarap Now that I had the knife, I had to find a hide with a heavy rear end the size of a pair of shoe soles. I found one and carefully cut the piece out. The knife was sharp. I stuck the piece of leather under my shirt and tightened my belt so it would not fall into my pants. The leather felt nice and warm against my belly. I got it safely into camp with no problem. The guards did not check us leaving the tannery. What could a guy possibly bring from there? I gave the leather to Bruno, and we dreamed of the bread we would buy with our rubles. He asked me more about what I did at the leather plant. I said I had worked in almost every department. A few days later he asked if I could get a pigskin. His contact would pay 150 rubles. That would get us five loaves of bread on the black market. The Russian population was still on bread rations. I turned the idea over in my mind. Yes, it was the thought of the bread. Money had no value to us—except for the bread we could buy. I didn't plan any of the details to get the job done. It had to be done spontaneously at the right location and at the right time.

One day, shortly before quitting time, I happened to be alone in the department where the pigskins were soaking in the oak tanning. Quickly I had a skin out of the pit, let it drip for a moment, folded it a couple of times, and fitted it perfectly under my shirt and pants. It was a little bulky, so I covered it with my army jacket. Our brigade met at the factory gate. I was in the middle as the guard counted us—only a seven-minute walk back to camp. The name of our brigade was called, the guard opened the gate, and the skin and I were on our way to 150 rubles. I could not believe it.

When most of the prisoners were in the dining hall, I put the skin under my mattress. My belly was darkened from the oak tanning. I waited for Bruno. He always came in late since it was quite a walk from his factory to the camp. He finally came. I told him I had the skin. He did not have to go to work the next day since his factory had a *vikbodnoi*, a shift-change day. That meant we had to leave the skin in our camp one more day. I did have to work the next day, so we moved the skin to Bruno's place where he could keep an eye on it. We stretched it out so it could dry a little better until the following day when we would take it out. That was the easiest part of the task. We would never be checked going out of the camp.

I dreamed about the bread I could buy. In the evening I ate only the soup, putting the slice of bread in my linen bread bag to eat just before going to sleep. That was so precious to me. We had it all planned. The next day after I came "home" from work, I lay down on my straw mattress and waited for evening soup time. Suddenly one of the guards from the front gate came in. That happened very seldom. He snooped around looking for something special, going from mattress to mattress searching underneath. I watched casually, acting disinterested. He came to Bruno's place.

"Ah, *tsap-tsarap*."

With those words, he pulled the pigskin out. He looked it over, folded it once, rolled it up, and walked out with a big smile. Most of the fellows in the room were surprised, as nobody had any idea what it was. I was scared someone would make a report to the tannery or make an investigation in the camp. Who had blown the whistle? The next day Bruno's brigade was sent to another job. He never came back to get paid for the leather for the shoe soles, or did he? I learned another lesson: Don't chew your bread until you have it between your teeth.

The next few days I went with mixed emotions to the factory. I was that special "good" worker. But how miserable I was! Nobody in our brigade had any idea how the skin got into the camp, and the stories got more and more colorful with each telling. The pigskin became a leather jacket. It grew bigger and bigger — a cowhide. It was fun to hear all the stories, knowing the facts, and then be silent. Anything different from the usual was welcomed.

The Escapee Returns Our interpreter took his job seriously, always with a stern expression. He wanted to please the Russian commander. He was the only one who could communicate with him and was therefore a very important person. He knew it and it showed. But today he was almost smiling. He could not keep it to himself any longer. The word was out: our runaway had been caught and would be delivered to the camp that afternoon.

Dead or alive?

At roll call our interpreter walked to the gate, opened it slightly, and our escapee entered. Had he been kept for this dramatic entrance? He stood in front of us, a bit shy, with a faint smile, not knowing how we would receive him. He had absolutely nothing with him when he left — just dressed in his uniform. How long ago? Three, four, five weeks? No one counted time. A single voice shouted:

"Welcome home!"

That broke the ice. He smiled more freely and waved his hand, as if to say: It is good to be back.

The interpreter exercised his "authority."

"This prisoner now has to live on water and bread only. He will go to work, but as soon as he is back in the camp, it's the slammer for him."

We did not know there was one. It was under the stairs to the upper room, a kind of a cage with meshed wire — exposed to weather and wind, with a dirt floor, long enough for a guy to stretch out, but only four steps high, not enough to sit straight up. On the high side of those four steps was the door — just a wood frame covered with mesh wire.

Tannery

The commandant was not present that evening. He came the next night, full of pride to explain to us that their system worked. No one could escape.

The poor guy was let out of his cell in the morning, got his slice of bread and bowl of water, and went to work with his brigade. Coming back at noon for lunch, he was locked up for the hour. Then back to work. In the evening, he went straight back to the slammer with only water and a piece of bread. This went on for more than a week, and then he was released.

He never talked about his experiences.

One day I must have caught him in the right mood. He told me his story from the beginning to the end. He said the worst part of his whole ordeal was being held in the guardhouse outside the camp until we lined up for roll call. He was captured by the police of a village and returned to Saratov. The guards in our gatehouse told him the other prisoners would beat him up as soon as he passed through the gate of the camp. Thus the reason for his shyness as he stood before us. Was this a tactic the Russians used to deter escapes? Were fellow prisoners "ordered" to carry out a punishment, to let their frustration be released? Was there an order given, but filtered out by the German commandant? Word never came to us. Would we have done it? We felt sorry for him, that he was caught and brought back to camp.

We called him Bert. Was it short for Albert, Robert, or Bertram? Bert painted his story in big strokes. Perhaps there were many painful details he did not want to talk about.

Where it all started or ended depends on how you look at it. Bert did not even know the name of the town where he was captured. He had jumped a train, but it later stopped and the engine was taken off. Since it would probably be a while before departure time, he sneaked off. A house close to the railroad tracks had an inviting vegetable garden. He thought he ducked low enough not to be seen from the house and was ready to grab some carrots, when out of nowhere a woman was standing before him, asking what he was doing there. She took him in the house and gave him a cup of milk and some bread.

"Homemade bread and milk. It's the best meal I have had since I was taken prisoner."

Before he could finish eating, two policemen came into the house, asked questions, and searched him. How did they know he was there? As he was led out, the woman winked, motioning him to take the rest of the bread.

They treated him fairly. He was kept in a makeshift jail. They asked him questions he hardly understood. He answered in his limited Russian. Those policemen laughed most of the time. What was so funny, he wondered? Someone came who spoke a little German. The police officer asked a question and the "interpreter" spoke in German, searching for the words. He acted like he did not understand his answer, asked a second time, and translated his answer very slowly. Bert had the feeling the man knew German very well but did not want the Russian officer to know. After almost a week, two soldiers guarded him back to Saratov in a passenger train.

During his escape he traveled by freight trains. Armed watchmen or soldiers were in every station. He had to learn the direction each train was headed, often waiting until an engine was hooked up to waiting freight cars before he jumped on. He saw other travelers like him, but avoided any contact. They avoided him, too. He walked or traveled mostly by night and slept by day — always on the alert, not to be seen. With an odd laugh, he said, "You learn to talk to yourself, but watch out when you start to answer to yourself."

It's not good to always be alone.

"I prepared my escape for about four weeks," he explained. He had saved two portions of bread every day and kept it hidden at the sawmill. But rats had found his cache. He found a safer spot, wrapped the bread in a piece of sack cloth torn from his stinking straw sack, and poured some old motor oil around it.

He worked at the sawmill where there were no restrooms, but plenty of bushes and high grass. When he had to go, he explored escape possibilities. He found a lot of openings in the fence around the mill — maybe for visitors to "find" some wood, boards, or whatever.

"One day there was a mix-up at the gate after our return to the mill from lunch. I walked out with another brigade, but got to my usual workplace. The count of every brigade was the same, day after day. Nobody would miss me in the count, and the other brigade came back with their daily number of prisoners."

He thought that was a good omen.

"And it was," he said with a laugh.

The first evening he hid in the high grass at the sawmill.

"I ate four portions of my stored bread. Never was I so full in all my prison days."

He paused, then continued: "I felt really good. Now I can face whatever comes. I am going home.

"Believe me, I will not try it again. It was hell. I became suspicious of every sound, every movement around me. It gets to you. I experienced the first calm moment when that woman took me into her house. I realized this was the end, but at least I could be human again."

He exclaimed, almost joyful, "It is good to be back. I did not want to talk about it. But now I feel better. It had to come out sometime. It is all behind me now. Do you understand?"

Nobody said a word. After a long pause, he said quietly, "I don't want to talk anymore."

Chess Some gifted guys carved a set of chess figures and made a chessboard out of cardboard. It was wonderful to play a game of chess in the evening hours. A second and third set were carved. One tried to outdo the other. My father taught me to play chess in my early teens, but I had not played for a long time. I liked the game — the mathematical thinking. It was a special treat on a warm evening to sit outside on a bench with the chessboard between us. Some of our guards watched us play and even challenged us to a game. The Russian medical sergeant in charge of the infirmary turned out to be a challenging chess player. He made an appointment to play with us the next day, at a certain time after his duties were finished. We got acquainted and played often together.

Often I could win the first game, but needed all my concentration to do it. If the loser wanted revenge, I no longer could concentrate. My brain burned out after the first round. This observation made our real condition very visible.

I wanted to learn Russian. Being in the country made for a great opportunity to learn the language. It was difficult. The Russians did not encourage us. We asked, but never received any text or study books. The words I studied and learned one day seemed to be lost the next day. It was a real struggle. My knowledge of the Russian language consisted of the words I heard on the job and from the guards in the camp. I got by. It was sometimes gesturing with hands and feet more than a conversation.

We discovered something interesting about the Russian language. Wolfgang was a good Latin student. If we could get a Russian newspaper, we tried to read the words. We could read the Cyrillic letters even if we could not pronounce them properly. Wolfgang pointed out to our surprise that many Russian words had a Latin origin. It became our entertainment to "read" something in Russian.

Far, Far Away In the evenings we could do what we liked within the boundary of the wood fence around us. I preferred to sit on the landing of the stairs leading to the upper room and look out over the Volga. In those days after the war there was hardly any ship traffic. When an occasional freighter came by, it caused a sensation. Many crowded the stairs to see anything moving on the river. I liked to sit and just watch the river flowing. I could "see" back in time, in location, longing for my wife, seeing our son, time we spent together, plans we made, and our dreams about the future. I remembered that before I proposed to Annemarie, I had asked if she would be willing to go to the United States after the war ended. One thing was for sure, and even stronger than before: I would do everything possible to make my dream of emigration to the United States a reality. I had been there before. In 1938 I crossed the ocean nine times as a ship photographer on the HAPAG S.S. *Hamburg*, but knew very little about the States. In New York I met friends of Waldemar's who lived in the New Jersey countryside, surrounded by forest with incredibly beautiful colors in the fall. I closed my eyes and had the picture before me — fall 1938. When I opened my eyes, I sat near the Volga River, fall 1946. I sat there and dreamed back and forth. Someday I will be in America with my family. I had been to countries that Hitler had not tried to conquer — Sweden, Switzerland, America. I compared the freedom they enjoyed to what the Nazis had done in Germany. I had always loved to explore the unknown, take chances, see new things — and, yes, take risks.

Here I was sitting on the stairs watching the river flow by. It never stands

I preferred to sit on the landing and look out over the Volga.

still. Drop by drop it becomes the water of this great river. The water from the north is the future. We cannot stop it — it's not static, it flows and it comes. What makes this misery bearable? Is it because it flows life? Why thoughts of hope? It came to me: Hope is part of faith — faith that this will not last forever.

A change for the better in the world can come only through change in the individual. That hope, rooted in the unknown, sustains us.

I felt peace deep inside me — peace with myself, my situation, my surroundings. It was bearable. Was I in harmony with the universe? Was I in harmony with God, the Creator of all things who gave me my thoughts? And my peace? I could not share those moments with anyone. I could not even make it clear in words. Maybe it was only for me. If I tried to tell someone my thoughts, they looked at me like: He has had it. He is on the brink of insanity. I was in harmony with what? With whom? I did not know. I knew only that I was not in turmoil. All was calm, all was so tranquil. I went straight back into the daily routine and did whatever I was told to do.

Our Real Enemy In camp we had only one enemy to fight. It was not the Russians. They were almost our "friends." They wanted maximum production out of us with as little of their input as possible. The lice we carried on our

Tannery

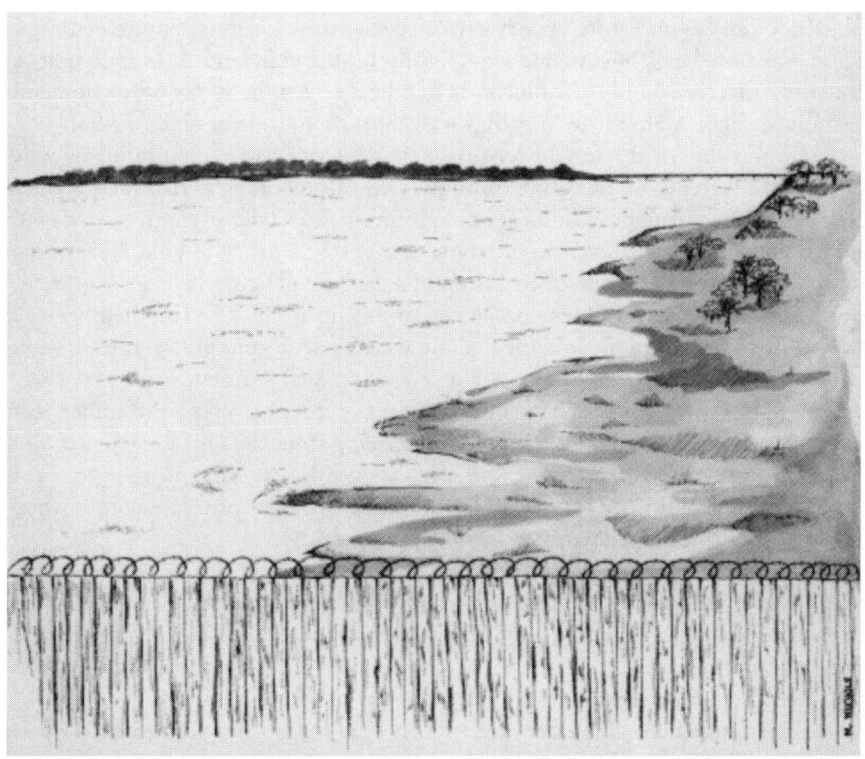

When I opened my eyes, I sat near the Volga River, fall 1946.

bodies — were they the enemy? We removed our shirts and searched for them. I remember seeing monkeys at the zoo searching and then crushing them with their teeth. In those happier days I had no idea I would get acquainted with those little creatures myself. If I found one, I crushed it between my fingernails similar to the monkeys. It makes a "clicking" sound, and I would go on to find the next. Where there is one, there are more. At least one could fight them.

The real enemy was the bedbugs. They nested in the sawdust that filled the outside walls of the building. It was now over a year since we arrived that first night. They sucked blood from all of us. There were times they did not bother me at all, and then they came to visit me in force. I was lucky, though, because my skin never swelled like some of the other men.

One Who Really Suffered Egon von Rège dropped the "von" from his name and was simply Egon Rège. In Russian, nobody could pronounce the accent grave on his name anyway. Egon was one of those who truly suffered from the bedbugs. I saw it every morning. He laughed about it, saying he inherited the blue blood of his ancestors, which gave a special treat for those Soviet bedbugs. Egon was not the strongest. He was slightly built, with reddish blonde hair, a face full of freckles, and light blue eyes that lit up when he spoke of his home in Hamburg. Egon wanted to do things well, but often was not able to do so.

He was one of the few lucky prisoners who still had a picture of his wife after all the searches we had gone through. I saw him looking at that picture, and the memories it brought back must have given him hope and strength from day to day to go through whatever might come. He still had his solid gold family ring with his coat of arms engraved in a deep blue lapis lazuli stone. He never wore it, but had it always well hidden somewhere in his uniform. The ring had been in his family for generations. It helped, along with his wife's picture, to sustain him.

We had to dress Egon every night, checking each garment to be sure there was not a bug already inside. We put a sack made from an old pair of underwear over his feet and hands, tightening it with a string from the outside. A mosquito net went over his head, fastened under his jacket. It was quite a nightly procedure. Nothing should have been able to get inside to bite him. How often when it was all done, and we lay down to sleep, Egon said:

"Hansarmin, there is a bug inside."

I had to undo him and trace the enemy to the area of his body that started to swell. Sometimes I got the bug; other times I didn't. I tied him up again, and he would always say:

"I hope I can sleep."

I imagined there were many nights he prayed for morning to come to release him from his torture. Egon suffered.

Never Again On Sundays most of us were in camp, and there was not much to do. The interpreter asked for volunteers.

"You will get bread."

Bread always sounded good. Why not? Going outside the camp was a welcome adventure; inside was just routine. He did not choose the weak ones from the many volunteers. He picked ten guys, including me, and we hopped onto a truck, not knowing what had to be done.

"You will see."

It did not sound too good. Anyway, it was good to be outside. We drove past the sawmill on a back road leading to the Volga. A barge was anchored on the shore of the river, with a plank reaching from the deck to shore.

From the gray dust on the plank, there was no more guessing. We would be carrying cement bags from the barge to the truck. We walked over that long plank as it whipped up and down, reached the deck, opened a deck cover and looked inside. Sure enough — cement! The bags were lying one deck below. No hoist, no crane — just ten guys, not too eager to lift those heavy bags. We were fools to volunteer, but now we were stuck. There was nothing to do but start and get it over with.

Carrying cement bags from the barge to the truck.

The first man loaded a cement bag on his shoulder. He had to get a good hold, balance carefully to make it up the ladder, crawl outside onto the deck, cross the heaving plank, trudge uphill to the truck and unload the bag. We decided right away that two guys would lift the bag onto the shoulder of the carrier. After he made the trip, two other guys helped in loading the next, and so in turn. No one had to stay too long in the cement dust on the lower deck. As the first man struggled with his bag, the plank whipped so much he almost fell off. We soon developed a better method: Two carriers would walk the plank out of step so it would stay down, not swing up, and two others would come back also out of step. Two did the loading inside. As the first man came up, he waited a moment for the second guy to walk the plank together. That gave a moment to catch a breath of fresh air — two over the plank, up the hill to the truck to unload. In the meantime two returned over the plank. So it went, snapping up round after round. With a system we could almost make a job fun. We were careful not to drop a bag inside the ship as the bag would burst and the dust would choke us to death. With the first bags we were careful not to get cement on our faces and under our collars, but after the second and third round it didn't seem to matter any longer. We looked at each other and complimented ourselves. We could laugh! Crying would have made things worse. We walked about ten rounds and said we needed a smoke break. After arguing for a while, they came up with the *makhorka* and the newspaper in which to roll the tobacco. We sat on the ground and smoked.

My first close encounter with the Volga was not very romantic. Each time I walked the plank I glanced at the river. I could see the flow of the water below. I wanted so badly to touch the water — just once.

Close by the barge we saw a pile lying near the shore. We walked over to it to relieve ourselves and saw many others had done the same. It was a pile of salt about five feet high. Through snow, rain, and sun, it had formed into a solid rock of salt.

We went back to our routine again. This time one of us searched for some ruptured cement bags. They were made of several layers of paper. The outside and inside layers would not be so valuable since they were covered with cement powder, reducing the trade value. But the in-between layers, if they were clean, would bring a good price. The paper was too tough for smoking. Someone had found that out already. But for the purpose of wiping yourself, it was very desirable. Back home we called it toilet paper. A layer from the midsection would probably bring up to three slices of bread; the outside layer would probably bring only one slice. The guys from the bakery brigade would have the most use for it, and they would be willing and able to pay the price.

The truck was loaded to its limit. It had taken two, maybe three hours. What is time in a prison camp? We dusted ourselves off, and I went down to the water to wash my hands and my face. I wanted to touch the Volga just once. It fulfilled the dream I had sitting on the landing of the stairs to the upper room.

The truck was too heavily loaded; it could not make it up the hill. We all pitched in, including the civilian, to give it that extra push to get it going. Back at camp we asked for our promised bread. The civilian shouted something to the gate guard.

"*Davai.*"

We were inside. That experience taught us another lesson: Do not volunteer for anything, and don't trust them no matter what they promise.

At least we had the proceeds from our paper sales and I had a chance to touch the Volga. I was happy.

Mail Arrived We got postcards nearly every other month to write our loved ones. We didn't believe it at first — mail actually arrived at our camp! The return cards we sent many months ago came back to us and there were even a few letters! The lucky prisoners who received mail from home never quit talking about it. The disappointed ones were a little envious. Maybe next time there will be something for us.

Little Ferocious Enemies Every six to eight weeks we were deloused. It was very tedious. Same place, same procedure. The lice never died. They just exchanged places. The temperature was not high enough to kill the lice. Our uniforms and underwear hung too close together for the hot air to get effectively in between, so the little critters went on excursions from uniform to uniform. After the pan shower with the smear soap, a procedure that by now we knew well, our garments felt good for a while until our new tenants began crawling on our skin.

On one of those trips for delousing, it was late and we were tired. As we dragged along back to the camp, the guard sergeant commanded us to sing to put life into the poor herd creeping along the road. The singing sounded awful. Very few of us even tried. It was pitiful. The sergeant stopped us and made it clear that either we sing the way we did in our own army or we would go double-time back to camp. We sang, and the singing did sound like the good old days. Maybe memories came back of times we sang those songs under more pleasant conditions. The response of the Russian civilians along the way was divided. Some smiled their approval. Others spit at our feet. We couldn't please them anyway.

No More Suffering It was late summer 1946. Time for a rear-end inspection again. Nothing new, always the same: give your name, drop your pants, turn around and show your rear, pull up your pants and walk out. If possible, you tried to catch what group they placed you in. Later Günther said I had come out in Group II again. He happened to be in the room when they called out the grading. I was on the borderline.

Egon Rège was in bad physical condition by this time. He was graded "D",— dystrophic. By now we knew they did not keep those "unworthy" ones in camp too long. They were given the opportunity of leaving on the next transport. Egon had not been strong from the beginning and now was worn out. With the small portions of food, we could not regain our strength. He was always willing to do his part, but even in the best condition he could not do hard physical labor. The nightly battle with the bugs did not help, either.

Not long after the inspection, word got around that a transport of the weak and sick ones would be leaving. Some who were scheduled to go home experienced a conflict—wanting to go home, but not wanting to leave their friends behind. Egon was worried about losing his signet ring during the many inspections he would go through. Guards searched the prisoners carefully before departing, taking whatever pleased them.

"Hansarmin," he said, "I want you to have this ring. If I keep it now, they will take it. If you ever find yourself in a bind, sell or trade it to survive. Feel free. If you can buy your freedom with it, let the ring go."

I did not want to take it. I didn't want the responsibility, but he continued:

"Hansarmin, do me this last favor and take my ring. You cared for me, always by my side when I needed someone. This is the last deed you can do for me."

We both had tears in our eyes. We hugged and cried as men do when emotions are overwhelming.

"I will bring it back to you, Egon," I whispered.

The moment made it hard to talk.

"Keep it," he pleaded.

"Stay in God's hand and make it home safely. And no more suffering."

These were the last words we exchanged. Names were called, Egon got into formation and walked out the gate.

That evening I sat for a long while on the steps leading to the upper room and watched "my" Volga flowing. In the distance I saw the water divided at the supports of the railroad bridge carrying tracks toward the Ural Mountains. The water united again, moving to the Caspian Sea. Evaporated by the sun, surface water becomes clouds and falls as rain to water seeds, to produce fruit. Nothing stands still. God created a fantastically beautiful universe. How few of us recognize it. What a blessing to be able to take time to be quiet. I went to my bunk to rest. I missed Egon. He was on his way home. I had peace. I thanked God that he would be safe now, no longer having to battle the ferocious little bedbugs. I had a good night's sleep.

Promises to Live On When we heard the rumor for the first time, we laughed: "*Voyna budit.*" (It will be war again.)

It was repeated every fall and spring in the years after the war. It was propaganda from on high to cover up an ailing economy that did not improve after the war. It was designed to convince the Russian people they were in a "worker's paradise." It kept the people in line, working and producing, demanding nothing for themselves — the working class. The war production industry did not seem to slow down after the Russian victory over Germany. The Russians were always hopeful fall to spring and spring to fall. When the new harvest came in there would be an abundance of bread. But there was never a plentiful harvest. Thus there was a shortage of feed for the cattle and very little meat on the table. Every spring, every fall, there was propaganda to explain why this or that was not available in the stores.

Since Egon was gone, I had no mission. I was used to wrapping him up for the night and experiencing happiness when he woke in the morning after a good night's rest. I hid his ring in my uniform. I wore my own simple wedding band and had never been bothered.

Plans for the Winter The days in the tannery again became a pleasant routine after the stolen hide situation. I swung around on those beams, hanging up the hides and changing their positions like a pro. I liked the job. Nobody pushed me. During the hot summer days, it was hot in the drying chamber. In the winter it would be warm and pleasant — a good place to survive the bitter cold Russian winters.

Handling those hides over the beams kept me in good physical shape, but reminded me how weak we became during those weeks sitting around in camp doing nothing — no physical activity, no energy. True, the nourishment was not good either. But how times had changed from those days of dried bread and a sip out of a can! Now three times a day we had three-quarters of a quart of hot soup with a slice of bread, at noon we even had *kasha*, and once in a while a little butter or sugar in the hand, and very seldom *makhorka*. I smoked for a while, then quit and traded tobacco for a slice of bread or some sugar. I was not hooked. It was good to have this "freedom."

Listless and Unresponsive After a big sip of stale water in a canteen at the tannery, I did not feel well. Eating was not enjoyable. I was not particularly sick, just miserable. One morning, Günther was at the gate watching the brigades going to their jobs. He saw me.

"Hansarmin, are you okay?"

He made a move to hold me back. But we were already counted and we marched through the gate.

I made it to my job, but I could hardly move. Everything seemed so heavy. Had I not realized how heavy those wet cowhides were? How hard it was to swing myself over the beams to get the hides up. I walked like an old man. Noon came, and I was thankful to go back to camp for lunch break — only a five- to seven-minute walk. Günther took me to the infirmary to check my temperature. I had a high fever. He sent me to my bunk and would call me when the Russian medical sergeant arrived for the afternoon. By the time he came my temperature was even higher, and he ordered me to the infirmary.

I don't know how many days went by. I did not care. Günther brought food the officers were served, but I was listless; I had no appetite. Oral medication did not change my condition. The medical sergeant gave me all kinds of shots in my buttocks. My temperature still did not come down. It hovered between 105 and 110 degrees. One day the sergeant put a needle directly into a vein in my left arm. His hands shook. Günther told me later that the shot was Salvarsan, a compound of arsenic used in those days against venereal disease. If he had not hit the vein, I could have lost all my hair and have had other complications. I was glad I had not known this when he injected me with shaky hands. Even this did not help and he finally gave up. He wanted desperately not to have to make a report of typhus in the camp.

I laid in a bunk in the same room where the patients stole those Christmas cookies back in 1945. I did not care. I had no desire for anything. Günther recommended that I be sent to the hospital. This medical sergeant and I had played chess together and we respected each other. Finally, he gave in and sent me to the hospital with typhus fever.

The Hospital

Ambulance Service Usually a patient had to walk accompanied by a nurse when he was sent to the hospital. I was not able to walk and went by "ambulance." The same little old man who drove the honey wagon came with his wagon without the barrel. It was one of those unpleasant fall days — windy, wet, and cold. They covered the bottom of the wagon with straw and a strawsack. I was dressed only in long linen underwear and a shirt. Günther covered me with an army coat and laid a blanket on top. We shook hands. The medical sergeant came, too, shook my hand, and said farewell. I thanked them both for what they had done for me as the wagon started up. The nurse walked on the side of the wagon and the old man encouraged his horse to keep going. My high temperature kept me warm.

Günther was the only one who knew Egon had left his ring with me. He had told me they would take it from me at the hospital, so I had hidden my wedding ring and Egon's ring in my anus. I had not eaten much in the last few weeks, so there was no danger I would lose the rings accidentally.

We finally arrived at the hospital for prisoners of war. It seemed forever.

The nurse had the order to bring the strawsack, blanket, and army coat back to the camp. As I walked into that hospital in my linen underwear, she waited for shoes (wooden soles and canvas cover). She took them from me as soon as I was inside the building.

A Lukewarm Welcome I did not have to be deloused, but was ordered to take a bath. I had to wait because the water was not hot enough, and I sat naked and shivering. The only thing I was allowed to carry with me was the little linen bag the *Calmuck* sergeant gave me the second day of my imprisonment and a spoon. I had to wait for the water to get hot. I sat naked with a shivering fit in that lukewarm bath — waiting, waiting. Finally a voice from somewhere told me I should wash in one of the pans. The water was lukewarm. I washed my upper body by pouring the water over my chest, then my feet and the lower parts by stepping into the small pan. How I got through the ordeal, I don't know. Somebody gave me a towel. What a luxury! The hospital "uniform" was a freshly washed shirt and long linen underpants. Someone led me up the stairs to a room. The only vacant bed was an upper one. I liked that, but could hardly climb in my condition. I finally got up on it, laid down and just wanted to rest: no thinking, no desires, zero, just lying there. I was exhausted.

Not long after, a sympathetic young Russian doctor came to check me out. He asked me questions:

"What caused your sickness?"

I did not know. I could only tell him I had had a high temperature for the past three or four weeks or longer. He looked me over, checked my lungs, and ordered me into another room. I was led to another room, one story below.

Next? The *starchi* (man in charge) looked me over and put me in the second-lowest bed close to the door. The person in the first bed was carried out the next morning dead. He figured I'd be next, and did not want to carry me the whole length of the room.

I got the rings out without too much difficulty and kept them in my hand. I wanted nothing, just to lie there. When the dinner soup came — mostly hot water — I ate two spoonfuls. I could not get any more down. I washed my two rings in the soup and told the *starchi* not to give the rest to anyone since I had typhus fever. I felt secure at the hospital and put both rings on my fingers.

At mealtime, I could not force myself to eat. I told the *starchi* to sell my bread and give me the rubles. My soup went to someone else. I looked forward to the nights to be left alone. The hospital must have been located close to the railroad yard. I could hear the whistle of switcher and train engines close by and far away. The sound of them reminded me of New York Harbor: tugboats, ferries, ocean liners, all sounding their horns. I was in another world.

Did I dream it, or was it the imagination of a delirium? A white airplane came into Saratov. I could see it from the hospital room. A friend of Waldemar, whose family I had visited on my trips to New York, came straight to the hospital and picked me up. My nights were full of such wonder and excitement. But then there was the reality of the day again.

The barber came to cut hair. He set a chair in the middle of the room about five feet from my bed. When it was my turn, I tried to walk to the chair. But my legs gave out. I was too weak. I sat on the edge of my bed and cried. I realized how physically weak I had become. Where were the times I swung the cowhides over the beams and carried those cement bags across the plank up the hill? How far away those days seemed! I did not eat. I had no appetite, no desire to live. I commended my family, my loved ones into the hands of God. I told Him to take care of them as He had taken care of me here in Russia. I wanted to die hearing the boat whistles in New York Harbor. What a beautiful memory.

A Piece of Bacon? One evening a man I knew from the sawmill camp came to our room. The *starchi* told him I would not eat. Paul had high-level connections that allowed him to leave the hospital and buy things at the bazaar: bread, milk, and kissly (a kind of half-evaporated milk simmered for days on the kitchen stove). He asked what I wanted to eat.

"Nothing."

I just wanted to get out of my misery, to get it over with.

Fairly late that evening, Paul returned. He was excited. He asked if I would like a piece of bacon someone had ordered but could not pay for. Bacon! A flash came back to me from my childhood. My mother in preparing a meal cut bacon into little squares. I always asked for a slice. I loved to chew on it. The German bacon in those days was mainly the white, fat part, a little smoked; delicious.

"Bacon!" I said. "I'll take it."

I had the rubles in my linen bag to pay for it. The *starchi* cut the bacon into little slices and put them on black bread. All of a sudden I wanted to eat again. I ate very slowly, chewing and chewing. It took me half the night. I heard the whistles of New York Harbor. It was music for my feast. That night I slept. The next morning I ate a bit more of my bacon and bread. That was the turning point. I continued to eat, and slowly my temperature came down.

Edmund Cord, a Berliner, came and visited me from time to time. Both being from the same city, we had much to talk about and became buddies. Edmund had had malaria and still suffered from fever attacks.

After Effects The right side of my buttocks was painful, especially if I lay too long on that side. On my first walk to the restroom, as I moved slowly along the hallway, I noticed I limped because of the pain. I must have looked dreadful, more dragging myself than walking. Someone asked why I was limping. I remembered I had gotten all the shots while in the camp infirmary on my right side, and this must be an after effect. He was a doctor, and would come to my room that night and take a look. I had completely forgotten and was surprised when he came by that same evening and checked me out. He had a pleasant personality. He was about my size, with dark hair and brown eyes that made contact with you. He was a person one could have confidence in as an MD. He thought I had an abscess from those injections, and suggested that it be drained. He could do it on a night when a certain nurse would be on duty. She had the key to the instrument and bandage closet. He would let me know what night.

A few nights later I was summoned to the surgical room. My doctor was with a Russian woman MD in the operating room. He waved that I should go back to my room. I limped back and waited patiently. I wondered what had happened. After quite a while he came, and we walked slowly back to the surgical room. Everything was prepared. He numbed the area with ether and a moment later had it open. The abscess was not fully developed and drained only a small amount of puss. He mentioned that he was sorry to have cut it too early, but at least it could now drain. He told me not to tell the Russian MD when she came to visit that he had opened it up.

Our lady doctor did not come until a day later. Everyone in the room had to come before her to be examined. When it was my turn, she looked at my bandage, which was pretty soaked by then, and told the *starchi* to get a nurse. When she came she gave her orders to put a new dressing on my spot. No questions were asked. I felt relieved. I did not know what to tell her anyway. My wound remained open, and it smelled as it drained very slowly.

Rumors, Blessed Rumors A rumor went through the hospital — some of us would be sent to a convalescent hospital where there was better and more food. Those who went there would be prepped before being sent home. What a story! A prisoner's dream — more to eat and going home, in one glad tiding. A few days later our woman doctor read the names of the men to be transferred to this special hospital in Atkarsk. That very afternoon we would walk to the train and leave the same night. She instructed the nurse to put a new dressing on my wound and said I would ride on a truck that takes the food to the railroad depot. They wanted to get rid of us in a hurry. We were issued uniforms, overcoats, a cap, and wooden canvas shoes. It was another one of those nasty, rainy fall days, and how good it felt to be dressed for a change.

Touching Only Our woman doctor saw to it that I got a seat on the supplies truck. Three other POWs and a nurse were already there, sitting on containers next to the cab of the truck. I had to sit on a crate in the middle. As we moved along, I stuck my hand into the crate and felt warm pieces of meat. But the opening was too small to get a piece of meat out. So I touched the meat many times and at least I could lick my fingers.

The truck arrived at a train of boxcars similar to those we rode into Saratov. I had forgotten how big the cars were and how high off the ground. It must have been the nurse's first time accompanying prisoners. She told us to get into the smaller car with the straw and mattresses and lie down. She and the driver unloaded the food boxes and crates. This beautiful nurse — she was beautiful to us for what she did — started feeding us with white bread and the warm meat I had been able to touch. We had never seen or tasted food like that since we were taken prisoner.

Standing Transport The other prisoners arrived later, walking slowly from the hospital to the train, and were assigned to the big boxcars. The guards and a doctor came to our car, and they made quite an uproar. The guards wanted to throw us out, but the nurse pleaded our case. We were in worse shape than any of the other patients. They argued back and forth. The soldiers won. They were friendly but firm, and they put each one of us in a different car to even out the number in each boxcar. By now it was night and pitch dark. There was no light even near the tracks where the train was standing. As I got out of our car, the mattress I was lying on just happened to get "glued" to my hands, and I carried it with me to the next car. I swung the mattress in first, then crawled in afterwards. None of the guards seemed to notice. It was puzzling.

The guys in the car had been there for quite a while and had stretched out and settled in. Then here comes a Johnny-come-lately, carrying his mattress. There were some unfriendly remarks. A familiar voice called out to me, indicating there was an open spot near him. It was Edmund, the malaria patient. We happened to end up in the same car. I recognized his full baritone voice in the dark. No one spoke like Edmund. Slowly and thoughtfully he expressed his views as he told a story. Edmund was a little taller than I, his blonde hair balding at the forehead. His face was long with prominent cheekbones. His blue eyes penetrated deep inside a person. When Edmund smiled, you could see that a couple of teeth were missing — which did not diminish the joyfulness of his smile.

There was enough room to spread the mattress on the floor. Our bodies were only skin and bones, and it would have been painful to lie on the wood floor. I told Edmund how the nurse had fed us four guys who had the privilege of riding on the truck.

We did not get anything to eat that night, nor did we pull away from the station. The convalescent hospital was only about fifty miles northeast of Saratov, where good food awaited us. About a third of the occupants in our car were Hungarians. Many of them did not speak German or Russian. There were very few Edmund and I could communicate with.

The next morning the guards counted how many were in the car. We each received a slice of black bread and about a third of the now cold meat I had received the night before.

We needed water to drink. After patiently waiting, we got one bucket full with the word it was to last. But for how long? Now we needed a bucket to relieve ourselves. Some of us still had diarrhea. The *vedro* (bucket) came and was passed around. There were fifty men in the boxcar. Someone called from a corner:

"I need the bucket."

There was urgency in his voice, but the bucket was on the other end of the car. A few minutes later, we heard the same voice, this time relieved:

"I don't need it anymore."

As the bucket moved around and filled up, it spilled on someone lying on the floor. At that point tension began to build up. We would have gotten into a fight and killed one another had not someone taken charge. He made us lie down at right angles to the long side of the outside walls. In that way we could crawl closer together and stay warm. The night was already getting cooler. It was October 1946. The way we were lying formed a walkway in the center, so the bucket problem could be handled without accident. The train did not move all that day.

That evening we each got a slice of bread and one little fish to be divided between three men. I passed it on. The meal from the night before carried me through. I wanted my share to go to Edmund, but he did not feel like eating, so the third man got the whole eight inches of fish. He said he did not care much for fish, but we noticed he ate it all. Things taste pretty good when one is hungry enough.

We asked the guards when we would be pulling out.

"*Nix machine.*"

They didn't know either. We spent another night there. Edmund woke up with a malaria attack. He was shaking. I covered him with my overcoat and laid close to him to keep him warm. He calmed down after a while and fell asleep. It was a blessing that we could share that mattress. Whenever I moved around too much my wound reacted. It was all wet and smelled terrible. Before night came we got a bucket of water. That night passed. We had not moved. We were still sitting on the same track as the night before.

Instead of breakfast came the promise:

"*Machine budit.*" (An engine will come.)

And the locomotive did come —*click, click, click.* I had not heard that sound for a long time. We started to roll. Let us go, let us go, let's not stop. Let's get out of this cold hell. I was not the only one who smelled bad. All of us had some kind of penetrating odor to share. We were in a state of apathy, not talking much. No more illusions, no more expectations; we wanted only to be out of there. The ride took just three to four hours. We arrived in Atkarsk on an overcast afternoon.

Atkarsk!

Born Again I was the last one to get out of the boxcar when we arrived at Atkarsk. I left the mattress. When one of the guards looked inside and saw it, he pointed at me to carry it out. I wondered if he knew that it stuck to my hands when I got put out of the officer's car, or was it just coincidence that he asked me to carry it? I had not planned to bring it with me to the hospital, but I did not mind. It was so much more comfortable for Edmund and me.

At the hospital the German staff, as well as the Russians, were waiting for us. They expected us two days before. We must have been an awful sight: dirty, stinking, hungry, and completely apathetic. We did not care. We had made it and that was all that mattered. Undressing was an eyesore even for us. How pitifully thin we were — skin covering bones. We went through the bath, and there was hot water in the showers! It felt so good to let warm water run down over our bodies. For most of us, it was the first hot shower we had had in years, towels to dry with, and the usual long linen pants and a shirt.

Edmund and I stuck together. We newcomers were directed upstairs into a large hall-like room with all the lights on. It felt like a friendly welcome. There were no bunks! Just one long continuous bed along the outside walls and two stretched through the center of the room. Mattresses were spread out on each cotlike base, with a neatly folded blanket for each man. It looked so inviting and made us feel special after what we had been through. Edmund and I chose a spot in the middle of the long bed, on the wall side opposite the window wall. It should be one of the warmer places. We laid down and felt we had experienced a new birth. As the room filled up, the *starchi* told us we should stay on our beds and food would be brought to everyone at his place. Tin bowls were neatly stacked and waiting to be filled and served. Two husky, heavy-set fellows came in with a steaming kettle of soup and a ladle. It looked like an often-repeated routine. The soup even had some substance to it. It tasted so good. The only thing I could almost compare it to was the *borscht* Silvertooth's wife served. How long ago that seemed to me now. Then came *kasha* and a slice of bread. It was like being in heaven. The discomfort of the last two days was soon forgotten. A new life had begun. This was a new world to explore.

The dressing for my wound was changed regularly, and with time it healed. I could walk again without limping.

House I and House II Two old school buildings had been converted into prisoner hospitals. House I, where we were assigned, was for more severe cases. House II, across the street, was for recuperating patients. Word spread around that some of the men from House I went home, but those from House II went back to the camps. Maybe there was a chance to go home.

Was this paradise on earth? We had nothing to do. Three good meals a day. Resting and sitting around on our beds, listening and talking, and hearing all the news filled our days. I met a man from another camp who had worked in a cement plant — unbelievable conditions they had to work in! I worked only about three hours carrying those cement bags out of the barge, but they toiled month after month with them. Many got sick. Many did not make it. The others were jealous of those who died, because whoever could still walk had to go to work. It was slavery. The Russians who worked right along with them were no better off. Other than a little more to eat, they were treated the same. How lucky we had been at our camp. The tasks had been nothing compared to those reports.

We had a pleasant bunch of guys in our corner. We talked about different subjects and told stories from our professions and our lives. Edmund was interesting to listen to. He was a fine baker of breads and delicious cakes and tortes. He had learned the trade from his father and knew it well. He had to start in the early morning hours. At 6:00 A.M. the loaves of different breads and rolls had to be on the bakery store shelves. In those days the apprentice delivered by bicycle to the neighborhood customers. People had roll bags nicely embroidered with their names hanging on the front doorknob. They wanted the fresh baked, crisp rolls early in the morning for breakfast.

Sitting on our beds, barefooted, just listening and talking, we discovered the guy next to us had only four toes. Someone asked the smart question, "How does it feel to walk on four toes?"

Maybe he was used to this question, because he replied, "I don't know, how does it feel to walk on five?"

We all had a good laugh, and no one mentioned it again.

We had baths regularly and looked forward to being under the shower. One time Edmund pointed to the bones sticking out in the back of our shoulders.

"Hansarmin, those are our angel wings. Someday we will fly home with them."

It put a smile on our faces, seeing us "flying" home.

Little White Mice *Chisty* (clean) was a regular word in the hospital. Six days a week between 11 A.M. and 4 P.M. for about an hour we had to be in our places, take off our shirts, and search for and crack lice. It became entertainment for us. A group of nurses, who were always talking back and forth to each other and ignoring us, inspected our shirts to see if they could find any more "homesteaders." They had more experience and knew how to find them. "*Nix, good comrade,*" they would say if they found one, and threw the shirt back to him to continue the search. We learned to look under and in the seams very closely, and sure enough, there they were. It was a daily game and almost our only entertainment. The nurses looked so cute in their white robes and head covers that we called them the "little white mice."

Sickroom I developed a temperature again. The woman doctor diagnosed pleurisy. I would be transferred into another room reserved for people who needed special attention and medication. This room had more serious cases. In the first bed was a young kid, quite ill. The woman in charge of the kitchen came in and stood by his bed.

"Oh, *Malinki, Malinki.*" (Oh, child, child.) "Do you want something special to eat?"

He did not. She had tears in her eyes as she went out the door. He died during the night.

Theo, the guy in front of my bed, had a funny habit. He would lie on his bed all day until the soup call came.

"Soup carriers out."

Then he would go into the stinking restroom and smoke his homemade cigarette. He did not come back until his soup was waiting and ready to be eaten. He did this at every meal. Perhaps his mother called him to the dinner table when the food was on his plate; maybe he liked to continue this homey habit.

I had been in this hospital room resting for two or possibly three weeks. It really made no difference. I had all the time in the world — no hurry, and it was a good place to be.

I was finally released from the room for really sick patients and sent back to the first room. I even got my old place back next to Edmund and my other buddies.

Heating Systems The heating system in our room worked on a simple theory. The body heat from eighty men in a room without any open windows created a warm atmosphere all night. But the next morning the air was so thick you could cut it into squares and carry it outside. The building had no central heating system, and coal or wood were not available. A "team of specialists" went out at night to the railroad yard and stole ties to heat the kitchen and bath.

Haven't Learned Yet Every other day a special group went to the warehouse with a wagon to get staple supplies for the hospitals. It was winter, but the day seemed so nice from inside. I volunteered for this duty since I was feeling so much better. Dressed in pants, jacket, a coat, and boots, I felt really warm until I went outside.

It was all downhill to the warehouse and no horse to pull the wagon, only six weak fellows. We hung on to the wagon so it would not run wild. Two guys steered it by the tongue. When we arrived, only the man in charge was allowed to go inside the warehouse. We had to wait outside. It was a sunny day, but we were cold — even leaning against the building in the sun. Incredible — 42 degrees F. below zero! That is just plain cold. We rubbed our noses so they would not freeze and walked in place to keep warm. Our clothes provided little protection against that kind of cold. There was not a layer of fat on our bodies either.

It's your own fault, I thought. You volunteered and here you are.

We waited for quite a long time before the supplies were ready to be loaded on our wagon. Then came the realization of why so many men were needed: to push that heavy wagon back up the hill to the hospitals.

This would be the last time I would ever volunteer for anything. I had volunteered for the cement bags. I should have known better.

The six of us had so little reserve it was a miracle we got that wagon up the hill. But we did. We unloaded the wagon, undressed, and turned in the uniform. I went straight to my bed and covered up to get warm. The extra bowl of soup we were promised for our labor did not come. That day there was no soup left over. That settled it — no more volunteering!

One day a medical inspection team came to the hospital. It was very informal compared to the routine in the camp. Our doctors knew us well, so we did not have to go bare butt. Only once in a while someone was asked to "drop his long johns" and present his rear end. The doctors picked some to be transferred to House II, the place for men who were getting well. I was one of those.

House II The House II building was cold. The rooms were much smaller. The only heating system was a huge free-standing stove that needed a lot of firewood. And there was never enough fuel to heat the rooms. Our beds were the same simple system as in House I, standing along three walls of the room. There was a straw sack for each, but the straw was packed down solid and hard. Still, it was some kind of insulation from the cold floor.

We could not figure out why our room was so cold until we discovered a layer of one-inch thick solid ice on the terrazzo floor under our bed structure. The windows were covered with solid ice all winter long.

One restroom was inside the building, but had only a urinal. The "real thing" was outside across the yard from the hospital. For that "run," three very light, worn-out gowns were provided. They hung in the hallway. If all three were gone, either you waited for one to be returned, or made the "run" just as you were, did what you had to do, and ran back to your bed, just about frozen to death. Fortunate were those of us who did not have diarrhea.

Three Under Three Our blankets, one per man, were so thin that daylight shone through. Also, our body heat went right through too. We learned very quickly to bundle three guys together, body to body, with three blankets on top. We laid like spoons on our sides with knees slightly bent. If one person wanted to turn, all three of us had to do it at the same time. We rotated positions so everyone had the middle position about every third night. It was the warmest spot. The system really worked. We stayed warm at least during the night.

My feet were so cold I could hardly feel them. One of the prisoners, Dr. Wisent, a German otologist who assisted the Russian doctor, visited me once in a while. In one of our many conversations I mentioned my foot problem. His diagnosis was poor blood circulation, and he ordered a foot massage every other day. Those massages worked wonders. For a time the feeling came back into my feet.

I thought coffee might help stimulate my blood circulation. I saved some of my bread portion, sold my tobacco, and had rubles to spend. A prisoner of war, who worked in the laboratory, arranged through a civilian to buy some coffee for me at the bazaar. The thought of having a cup of coffee once in a while was exciting. The package contained more chicory than coffee. The guy in the lab brewed it a couple of times and we sipped it together. But he did not want to risk his job, and I was stuck with my chicory coffee. I ate a spoonful now and then, but my feet were still cold most of the time. No wonder, the temperature outside stayed at minus 40 degrees, and the buildup of ice on the terrazzo floor made our room worse than hell. Sometimes I wished it were hell instead of our "deep freeze." At least we would be hot. Dr. Wisent visited me more often, and we spent hours in stimulating conversation. How refreshing!

With the Help of the Sun Spring must have been right around the corner; the days turned slowly longer. I noticed a little pimple on the top of my left shoulder close to my neck. I observed it for a couple of days. I could not see it without a mirror, but I could feel it. One beautiful sunny day, it warmed up a little, and I stuck my shoulder through the open window to let the heat of the sun penetrate that spot. It felt so good to enjoy the warm sun's rays falling on my shoulder. I felt something was cooking inside the pimple. Within a couple of days the little pimple developed into something bigger and I ran a light fever. Here came my chance. The next day I was transferred back to House I.

Back in Paradise What a change! I had forgotten what a joy House I was. It must have been the older of the two buildings, with a decorative wrought iron staircase railing that led to the second floor. It had a wood floor throughout that made the house so much warmer than House II with the frozen terrazzo floors. I was assigned another room, a smaller one, with maybe thirty-five patients. It was cozy and warm. I was familiar with the surroundings and the schedule. Not much had changed since I left. It was good to be back.

Within a few days, I was scheduled for surgery. My little pimple had grown into a good-sized boil. Dr. Rued, a well-known surgeon from Erlangen, performed the operation. It left quite a hole in my shoulder. My treatment had worked for me to return to House I. I was a new face to the occupants in my new room, but they welcomed me and soon we were friends. It was like heaven on earth compared to the deep freeze in the other building. The same food we had in the other place was served here because it was cooked in one kitchen. But it tasted better! It was a special place for really sick German prisoners of war.

A Message to Home Transferring from the camp to the hospital in Saratov and then to Atkarsk, I had not received any mail. When we received postcards to write home again, I had new hope that I would get an answer from my loved ones eventually, or at least they would get a message from me. The rules were very strict. We were not allowed to write more than twenty-five words. What should I let them know in those few words? I formulated my message many times in my mind. Finally, I wrote:

"Dearest Annemie, greetings from best condition and recovery. All my thoughts to you and Hans. Stay patient until I return. We're in God's hands. Love to all, Hansarmin." I stretched out the twenty-five words by not counting the address and the signature.

A *starchi* was in charge of keeping the room clean and in order, and seeing to it that everyone got his food and medication. He was also the interpreter for the doctor and the patients. He did just about everything. Two helpers carried the soup and the *kasha* to the men on their beds, as well as distributing the bread and cleaning the rooms. For their efforts, the room *starchi* and his helpers got an extra bowl of soup if there was some left. The rest of the leftovers, if any, would go to the patients, room-to-room, in a precise order. There were always watchdogs who knew exactly how far second helpings should go in a certain room and who would get served next and how much there would be left. The starchi in our room must have been doing the job for some time. He ran his duties smoothly and was well fed.

Changing of the Guard Some of those well-fed guys (who were German prisoners) were transferred to House II. We had lost our *starchi*. During her next visit, our doctor asked one of us to volunteer for the job. No one responded. To be honest, it was work, and the *starchi* was always between patients and the authorities. The doctor began asking the men she had known for a long time. Everyone declined. In her dilemma she turned to me. I was new in the room and was just ready to say "*Nyet*." Someone said:

"*Da*, Schuetz."

They all shouted:

"*Da*, starchi."

The doctor was pleased to find someone the patients accepted. I became the new *starchi*. It was a job I had to learn, with a lot of challenges.

The biggest privilege I had as a *starchi* was a free-standing bed all to myself. That night I felt the whole world belonged to me. I stretched out and turned around on that bed as much as I pleased. There were no longer three guys lying under three blankets like spoons, clinging to each other, and changing positions on command.

With all of my chores and duties, I kept busy. The first half of each day passed so fast that in no time it was noon. When they sent the well-fed prisoners to the other house, all of the helping hands were gone. House I was really short for many chores. There was not enough help to distribute the soup and *kasha*. The commander of the hospital came to my room and told me to help in giving out the food. He didn't ask — he ordered! I told him straight out that I could not carry those heavy pots. He agreed and gave me two men to carry them. But I would be responsible for giving it out. I had to hustle in order to get that first noon meal served.

I quickly learned what was called the "tempo," the number of portions expected to come out of one pot. That was no problem with the soup — one ladle full to each patient, about three-fourths of a quart. That quota could always be reached by adding more water if necessary right in the kitchen. It was important to keep stirring the soups so what little solid substance there was would be distributed evenly.

The soup serving started with the call, "Soup carriers out." It was the signal for mealtime. I went to the kitchen for a serving spoon and a ladle. If there was plenty of soup, I was to serve a full ladle to each man; if short, I had to cut the amount.

The *kasha* was more critical. If the tempo was called fifty, it meant I had to give fifty portions of *kasha* out of the pot. It was important that everyone was served. The first couple of times I was nervous. I tried my best to be fair in serving everyone equally. I remembered every pair of eyes had watched the previous servers, as I had myself. Now the eyes were upon me.

I went to my room exhausted. I was under so much pressure to do the serving right I could not eat my soup. I gave it and my *kasha* away.

Someone from the kitchen brought me another bowl of soup and kasha for my service. I did not know I would get paid in "extra" food for my work. I gave it to the men lying close to my bed.

I wanted to go home and knew I had to stay slim and frail to do so. If I gained weight I would be moved to House II and back into a camp to work.

I figured it all out. I ate only my regular meal. Any extra I gave away — some to a friend who was in bad shape, or in rotation to the men in my room. My extra food was unbelievable: like every prisoner I had a regular meal, then additional soup as *starchi*, and on top of that, soup and *kasha* direct from the kitchen for my service. I made a lot of friends! I did not want to gain one ounce. Staying slim was the only sure way of going home. The busy days passed quickly. It was wonderful.

Pleasant Visitors Every time, before the doctors came to visit, the "little white mice" made their inspection of our shirts for lice. I took my shirt off, as all the men did, searching for and cracking lice. This made a deep impression on the men and encouraged them to search more extensively for the critters. Soon our room was lice free. Not finding any, the nurses went out satisfied and smiling.

"*Khorosho palata.*" ("This room is okay.")

Valkyrie Our doctor was an attractive woman. Her appearance alone gave her authority. She was tall and not too slim, with blonde hair, blue eyes, and light pink skin. She looked directly at you when she talked and really listened. If her hair had been dark, she would have been the perfect Valkyrie. I gave her that name — Valkyrie. She was truly a gentle woman. She had compassion for us. But the whole system was rotten. Still, it felt so good that someone cared. It could not change the conditions, but for sure it soothed the situation.

She kept records of every patient in our room. The paper that she made the reports on came from pages torn out of books and stitched together by a thread. She wrote her reports in Russian handwriting at a right angle to the printed text on the pages. It was amazing how easy it was to read. She sat at a little table and asked each patient:

"How do you feel? Has anything changed since our last visit?"

I translated the questions for her from Russian to German, limited as it was. Fortunately, the men always answered the same: weak, sometimes dizzy, light-headed, hungry. If anyone complained about discomfort, she would look him over, make notes, check his heartbeat and lungs. Sometimes she prescribed some medication or even shots. It was an excellent relationship we had with her. She won our confidence. We knew she did as much as she could for us. When she was finished with all the men in the room, she sometimes looked at me and asked:

"And how are you?"

I said only "*Khorosho.*"

She smiled at me.

"*Khorosho.*"

This one at least felt good. And I did. I was so occupied all day with my responsibilities, and mealtimes came so quickly that I did not have time to even think about being sick. Being usefully occupied is the best therapy.

Another World

Night Visits The German officers and the MDs had a room to themselves. They had individual beds that were not so crowded and the room had a pleasant atmosphere. They received the same hot meals as the other patients. I served them the same size portions that I dished out in all the other rooms.

I got more acquainted with Dr. Wisent and Dr. Ruad. We greeted one other in the hallway, and one day they invited me into their room. We sat very casually together and talked about old times and our experiences — whatever came up. I felt quite honored to be included. I looked forward to those visits, especially hearing more interesting things than the old WP stories. At first I listened, but later shared about my life. They enjoyed an outsider's new stories. I talked about my goal in life: to someday direct movies. I told them about the tank battle films I had created, as well as a film we made earlier with Gustaf Gruendgens, who was a famous actor and director when I was an assistant camera man. We had to travel to Babelberg Studios in Berlin to see the scenes from the previous day. On the way back to our hotel on the outskirts of Berlin, where we did the actual filming, I rode with the producer. We stopped in Potsdam for a late dinner. I was young and fairly new in the film business. It was just before the war. He told me very frankly not to get involved with girls in the movie industry:

"Stay out of those circles. They bring only gossip and create bad working relations."

I followed his advice.

To them, my experiences were a bit out of the ordinary — definitely different. I also talked about moviemaking tricks that were common and artists we all knew with whom I had worked. It brought back beautiful memories and lifted my spirits. I looked forward to those evening hours after my duties were done. It was like having a private life again.

The Key to Going Home On one of those evenings, someone made the remark:

"Why don't you gain any weight? You are a *starchi* and get all those extra servings."

I was honest.

"I have a plan to go home from this hospital by not gaining any weight. I give away the extras I get, eating only my normal portion like everyone else."

They thought it was a good plan if I could stick to it. They did not know I thanked God before and after every meal, that I ate whatever I had and was filled. This relationship with my God worked out very well.

We did not visit every evening. It was a loose relationship. But those hours we did spend together were like stepping into another world. A lawyer from Goslar, Reiners, had stories about divorce and other interesting court cases. He told us that the court had an unwritten rule for married couples. Quoting Martin Luther, the reformer: "*Die wochen zween, macht im Jahr 104, das schadet weder ihr noch dir.*" ("Twice a week makes 104 a year, that is not bad for him, or for her.")

My View Sometimes I was very frank and shared my thoughts, especially concerning Hitler and the Nazi Party. I had been convinced for a long time that Hitler started the war because Germany was bankrupt. Most of the people did not want to believe this, as the war made things appear to be better in Germany. In 1932, seven million were unemployed and the economy was just creeping along. In 1933, Hitler came with his grandiose ideas. Yes, he created jobs, built up the army, the air force and the navy — all very expensive projects without a return. Soldiers cost money but do not produce. Building the autobahn, four-lane highways, big party buildings — all were investments with no returns. True, it put people to work. They were able to make a living and pay their taxes. Through payroll deductions many saved for a Volkswagen beetle, an automobile that could be bought in 1938 for under a thousand marks ($400). Hitler built the automobile factory with their savings, but nobody got a car. As the beetle production began, the war started — it was perfect timing. The plant was then needed for war production.

The German people had money to spend, but who paid for the "improvements" in the first place? The government. But the government is the people — you and I. The presses had to speed up the printing of worthless money. It devalued the mark in trade with other countries. It was not noticeable right away within Germany, but it eventually devastated the economy.

I remember on my return from New York as photographer on the S.S. *Hamburg* that I wanted to be home for my mother's birthday on February 21. I took the *Flying Hamburger*. In those days it was the fastest train between Hamburg and Berlin. It cost only a small amount more, but I enjoyed the ride — every kilometer. I happened to read the *Frankfurter Zeitung*, a reliable business paper in those days. A very small note caught my eye. Germany had sold so many thousand tons of coffee to Denmark. Later I called a friend in Berlin who had knowledge about our economy and the trades. I asked him what it meant. He explained that Germany delivered goods to Brazil, took coffee in trade, then traded the coffee for something from Denmark. To make it more lucrative for the Danes, we offered it below world market price, which meant somebody had to pay the difference in value. How long can a nation trade like that and not go bankrupt? Well, Germany was getting close as 1939 approached.

On those trips to New York, the freight from Germany was only bags and boxes of emigrants who were allowed to leave and take their belongings. But the freight from New York to home was scrapped blocks from smashed cars. The German Nazi press did not print that no nation would sell us valuable raw materials. With the persecution of the Jews, Hitler really started to dig his own grave. It was well known that big business and trade go through Jewish merchants at some point along the line. The Jews, without a nation of their own, always supported their own people. Since *Kristallnacht* in 1938, they had boycotted products made in Germany. It backfired on Hitler, who must have suffered from megalomania. No, he did not suffer. He enjoyed it and thought he had all the people behind him. "*Führer befiel — wir folgen?*" ("Führer give the order, and we follow.") But I saw in the bomb shelters during the air raids when the earth shook from the allied bombing, suddenly in fear and trembling, people fell on their knees and prayed like they had not done for a long time. If one could take a leap from January 1933 when it all started to this moment, who would have believed it? How gradually we slid into it.

The Act of Providence When Hitler's life was spared in the assassination attempt on July 20, 1944, he proclaimed in his arrogance that *Vorsehung* (Providence) had protected him. This statement was the only truth he ever expressed. He had to go to the bitter end of a lost war for the "good of the German nation." If Hitler had been killed in 1944 and the war had come to an unpleasant end, then many people would have said for a long time: "We lost the war, but if the *Führer* had lived, it would not have happened."

Hitler would have been an idol forever. I believe in a righteous God who spared Hitler to bring him to the tragic end — the same as he brought on this nation. That was the price Germany had to pay to get rid of the monster.

There was silence for a long time. My thoughts could come out in the open again. There in a prisoner of war hospital in Russia in 1947, I let it all come out. I had no hate, only deep sorrow for what one man could do to a nation. Maybe the dream I had had from my teens, an idea that started after World War I — the Pan-European Union — could now be possible — that the nations would come together as a United Europe similar to the United States. If this war led to that, then it would not have been fought and lost in vain.

It was late, and I had talked too much. Nobody argued. I said good night and went to my room. Everyone was sound asleep. I silently recited, "Father, Thy will be done in what the day brings tomorrow."

And I slept soundly.

The next day I got up early and checked to see that the men got to the washroom. I had to have the room cleaned and ready for the "little white mice" and Valkyrie when she came for her visit. It was always the same routine. One day she asked me if I knew English. "*Da.*" Yes, she needed my help! That puzzled me. Does she work for the underground? It went through my mind all day.

At noon, the call for soup carriers came, and I went to serve.

Carvers' Corner In our room there were some talented craftsmen. They were always busy and calm, content with whatever they got or had. Our room had a pleasant atmosphere because of these men. It was my "kingdom," but I was there to serve the others and I liked doing it. In return, time passed quickly. We had respect for one another and made allowances for each other. There was never any yelling. We could laugh and joke together. We lived with the hope of eventually going home — someday.

Summer passed quickly. The craftsmen carved smoking pipes and little flutes. One person worked for months putting together a weaver's loom, a miniature about eight inches square. Valkyrie was so impressed that she brought every Russian to our room to have the loom demonstrated. She was in charge of this room, and it seemed like her own accomplishment.

Two days later Valkyrie brought me the instructions for penicillin, which were written in English (manufactured in the USA). She did not understand a word, and I was of very little help to her. The instructions talked about one hundred thousand units and other numbers. Finally I interpreted a section that indicated the serum was for injection. I tried to explain it in my limited Russian. We gestured and talked to each other. I hoped I had helped her and someone in need of penicillin could benefit from it.

There was a wonderful story about penicillin: Someone had found a fungus on the basement wall of a damp cellar in Moscow and penicillin was discovered. It was a Russian discovery.

Going Home? Rumors spread that a committee would come soon, examine the men, and decide who should be sent home. Here was the chance I had been waiting for. I organized my room for their arrival. Everyone would be identified by his name and the right man with his illness. Valkyrie explained every case to the members of the committee. Every man in the hospital was required to go through the inspection and then wait anxiously for the results. Two days later about one-third of the patient reports came back. I sorted the papers very quickly. It looked like the men whose reports did not return would have a chance of going home. My report did not come back. What excitement there was throughout the hospital! Even those who knew they had no chance of going home were glad some men would be shipped out. It gave hope that someday the turn for all would come. Within a week we received confirmation on those men who would be on the next train home. I was on the list! My plan had worked! I had given away all those extra meals and had not gained any weight.

I had beaten the system! In three weeks we would leave. I figured one week on the train, so in about four weeks I would be able to take my wife in my arms and see our son, Hans, who was now five years old. The expectation was almost unbearable. Many of my buddies were on the list.

Valkyrie made her visit and we went through those men whose papers had come back. She looked at those who would be going home and smiled. She looked at me and asked, "How about you?"

"*Damoi.*" ("Home.")

She teased me: "You? You also?"

But she knew because she was the main influence on the committee. She seemed satisfied that so many from her room would be going home. Valkyrie must have known what is meant to be away from loved ones. She was really a caring physician and did well with the limited medical supplies. She was a passionate woman. Those going home received new underwear, fairly good uniforms, socks — which we had not had for years, and canvas-covered shoes with wooden soles. In two weeks at the latest we would be home. The day finally came, and we assembled in the courtyard. The German commander read our names and said, "This is your railroad ticket home. Good luck to you. I hope we also will be home soon."

With those words, we turned and walked toward the gate.

Called Back I walked close to the rear and was just about to take the last step through the gate when a nurse appeared at the door of the hospital building and called:

"Schuetz."

I looked at her thinking I had forgotten something. She ran toward me with tears in her eyes.

"*Davai, nasard.*" ("Come back.")

Why? I hesitated. She took me to the doctors' conference room on the lower level. The chief physician of the hospital — a dear, motherly type woman — looked at me as if to say, What happened? Puzzled, I asked, "Back! But why?"

She said only, "I don't know."

But then it came to her — NKWD. She held her hands to her head as if to say, "This is out of my control."

I stood paralyzed. The lieutenant of the NKWD — the secret police — came down the stairs waving some papers.

"Khansarmin Schuetz?"

"*Da.*"

"*Davai palata.*" ("Go to your room.")

I went back to that room I had left just two hours before. What had happened? The news went like wildfire throughout the hospital.

"Hansarmin is back. The lieutenant did not let him go."

My dear friends gave me all kinds of good advice. One guy wanted to kill the lieutenant. I wanted only to be left alone. The turmoil finally calmed down, and I was by myself.

The Promise That night I prayed:

"Father, why is it that I could not go home? Was it that I am not fully prepared? Are my loved ones not ready to receive me?"

I did not argue — I was too numb. A deeply silent but clear voice from within came:

"Hansarmin, *in the fullness of time* you will go home. *No matter in what condition you shall be.*"

Oh, how I wished I could continue to hear that voice, but that was all. I was exhausted and fell into a deep, restful sleep. The next day I felt ashamed to be the only one who could not go with the others. There were many questions, but I had no answers. I never found out why I didn't get to go home.

One thought came to me later. When I was visiting in the officers' room where we talked freely, there was one guy close by lying on his bed, just listening. He never took part in our conversations. Was he there to listen and report?

Engels

Return to Reality Within a few days, all Group III prisoners were on the next train out. How glad I was to leave. To be called back was a cruel disappointment. My plan to stay thin so I would be allowed to go home did not work. Someone higher had a better way prepared for me.

"*No matter in what condition you shall be.*"

I remembered the still quiet voice within, and from that day on I ate everything I could lay my hands on. I knew one thing for sure: There will be a fullness of time that will take me home.

We rode in the usual boxcars for three or four hours, our destination unknown. I don't think the guards knew where we were going either. One exciting part of the trip was the long bridge over the Volga close to Saratov — the bridge I could see from the stairs at the camp. We crossed the Volga! That hollow sound under the open railroad tracks was music to my ears. The train went slowly over the bridge. I heard every click where two rails met. That sound provided "food" for all kinds of speculation. Maybe we were going to Siberia, the Urals. We had not seen any trip supplies loaded on the train. Strange. Maybe an hour after the bridge crossing we came to a stop. It was the end of our travels. We had arrived.

First Impression Climbing out of the cars, we noticed a good-sized factory complex in the middle of nowhere. What kind of production went on inside this complex? We got in formation, were counted, and walked along the factory fence to a camp about a five-minute walk from the plant and surrounded by no-man's-land. There was an open-mesh fence with barbed wire on top and the usual watchtowers on the four corners were the boundaries of the camp. We could see through the fence, through the camp, and out on the other side. There were no buildings inside the camp, only dirt mounds protruding from the ground — not very inviting. So that was it. Walking through the gate we passed under a sign that read, "Welcome to Camp 14." It was a nice, warm fall day, and we enjoyed standing in the open to be registered one by one.

"Give your name, birthdate, profession if you have one, or the kind of work you have done before."

Suddenly many of us were cooks or bakers. We were divided into the different earth-covered, half-underground quarters. It wasn't too bad. A couple of steps led down to a good-sized room with a wooden floor and units of four bunks — two low and two high — so everyone had an individual bed with a straw sack. It was almost as comfortable as the hospital. Small windows let in little light, but lightbulbs hanging down from the fairly low ceiling made for a cozy atmosphere.

We were on the east side of the Volga, close to the town of Engels. The plant was a freight-wagon factory. The old-timers said the food supply was fair and the working conditions were okay. We could learn to live with them.

In the dining hall, soup awaited us. It appeared to have been made of leftovers from the noon meal. It was hot, and we got the usual slice of bread, which was always a welcome part of the meal.

Four-Hour Shifts We were all Group III men, but things had changed during the one year I was in the hospital. Group III men worked only four hours a day. We were divided into brigades. The first shift was from 8:00 A.M. to 12:00 noon, with afternoons in the camp. The second shift was from 1:00 P.M. to 5:00 P.M., with mornings in the camp. That did not sound too bad. Individuals with the best chance of getting a satisfying job were specialists in machinery — anyone knowing about machine repair or machine operation. The WPs could actually earn rubles. A certain amount of that money went toward room and board. A prisoner would be paid 85 percent of any amount above that, up to 150 rubles per month. The system was unheard of by anyone. With four hours of work per day, we would never reach even the minimum to cover camp costs. With an eight-hour shift and a special skilled job, one could earn a few rubles. Still, it was quite different from conditions a year ago.

After a good meal of soup and hearing all the camp news, I was ready to go to work and see for myself how the system worked. I chose and was assigned to the morning shift. That would give me afternoons to spend at the camp library, which had many books by Lenin, a few by Pushkin and others in German print, and old East Berlin newspapers. What an improvement!

Ready to Work The next morning we left early enough to be at the plant by 8:00 A.M. We had to wait for orders. Whoever was in charge was not prepared for so many workers. Some were assigned to help a Russian worker move parts produced by a machine, others were ordered to clean up. The whole plant needed a good cleaning. I had the impression the plant had many hands but no head to give direction and make it productive. Working under those conditions for days, I observed how work got done. It was a large plant that built special railroad cars, with metal sidewalls open on the top for loading and chutes at the bottom for unloading.

We were divided into five brigades, with one head brigadier in charge. He had quite a job organizing the WPs every day and implementing those two four-hour shifts. The men who worked in the afternoon did not know what the others had done in the morning. The head brigadier sometimes assigned different jobs for the afternoon shift. With that system, nothing much ever got accomplished.

One day after weeks had passed, Willi Rausch, the head brigadier, asked me to be a brigadier. He had observed my work and thought I would be the right man to handle the job.

"No way," was my answer. "I don't speak good enough Russian. I'd rather do what I am told to do than to be responsible for others."

Then Franz Hege, the Group III brigadier with one of the four-hour shifts, begged me to help him with his workload. One man could not handle sixty to eighty men on a job site. Then Willi asked me again. He would help me. He said I would learn and catch on quickly. He would give me the brigade with the best workers. It was a real mess — nothing was organized and they did need help.

On-the-Job Training Finally I gave in, not knowing what I was getting into. I learned the system as I went along. Slowly I got the picture.

Taking the brigade to the plant and assigning men to different duties was the easiest part of the job. The fourth brigade had many specialty workers who had been there a long time and knew the ropes. Some worked on a lathe and made good wages. Those guys saw to it that they got their *naryads*. They were paid by the piece and knew exactly what they had coming. No *natchalnik* or foreman could short them. Those men were the bread and butter of the fourth brigade.

Two other men managed to do their own bookkeeping, too. They moved the railroad car wheels from a special lathe to the assembly line where they were installed to the undercarriage of the freight cars. They swung those wheels from the lathe, set them up, and rolled them like toy tops to the undercarriage assembly line. Even the Russians were impressed with the way the two guys handled those heavy steel railroad wheels. Both were husky fellows. They worked for a long time in the camp kitchen, washing pots and pans and doing other odd jobs. I assumed they ate as much as they wanted. Only with that supplement could they perform the work they did in the plant.

They were a solid base on which to build a brigade. I learned that for every job completed, however small it might be, I had to get a *naryad* document to prove our work and performance. The *naryad* showed the department where the work was performed, the work done, how many workers, the percentage of the normal performance, and the rubles earned. I was warned some of the department heads would try to short us. What do *vojeno plenys* know? To stand up to them for my men, I would have to improve my Russian language skills. It had gotten me by in the hospital, but not anymore. I needed a completely different vocabulary.

My specialty workers helped me tremendously: what to ask for, what to watch for, and where to get the right documents.

They taught me to read what was written on the documents. Among other things, I furnished men for "transport" in order to move material from one production place to an assembly line in another department. The most difficult part of this job was to get the right credit for the work performed. One department pointed to the other to write the *naryad* for paying the bill. The men worked hard, but seldom did we get the credit we deserved. In the past, nobody was in charge. The foremen took advantage of that fact and cheated the men out of their earnings. The foremen of the different departments soon learned I was in charge of who would be working for them. It took awhile, but I made them understand that even though we were WPs, they should not take advantage of us. In the past years of our imprisonment, the Russians could get anything done for a talon, a meal, a piece of bread, or for nothing. Things had changed drastically.

Sometimes I told them off in my broken, stumbling Russian. In their eyes the WP may not be worth much, but they soon learned we would have to be reimbursed for our work. In my first confrontation I made some of the *natchalniks* angry. To be honest, I was scared about how I measured up. The effect was fantastic. The foremen respected me from then on. It established a good basis for our work relationship. They knew every man transporting material would have to be reimbursed for his work. It was hard to control since I was not always around to check what the men had actually moved, and there was no pencil or paper for keeping count. I said to the men:

"Scratch it on a piece of scrap metal. There's plenty of it lying around."

Bookkeeping As brigadier, I collected all *naryads* at the end of the month and began the long nights of bookkeeping. I divided the *naryads* so that all the men got their fair share. I filled in the papers with the name, percent, and the rubles. The end amount had to be correct. The best workers on those special jobs received their limit of 150 rubles, but their earnings above that amount would have been lost. Willi helped and showed me the tricks as he said he would. I just transferred the percentage and rubles to those men who, through their job assignments, had no chance to earn anything. And they worked as hard as anyone else. I don't know if it was legal. It was earned by men within my brigade; I only distributed it evenly. I did not have an abacus and wouldn't know how to use one anyway. Besides, I did not have enough paper to make the calculations before I had to put the final figures in the report sheet. I concentrated on my work because the figures had to be correct. I was glad when I finished it the first time. The morning soup and bread tasted twice as good that day.

Two more men belonged to my brigade. One was an engineer and the other was a technical draftsman. They were treated like employees on the payroll of the engineering department. Those two saw that the *naryads* were correct and on time.

At the end of the freight car assembly line was the main inspector who finally inspected every car. If it passed, the car was counted toward the fulfillment of the five-year plan. Supreme Soviet departments set up five-year plans for the whole country and for all kinds of production and harvest. Everything was regulated from Moscow. They didn't know much about the different conditions of soil, weather, when to plant or harvest, but it was all planned in departments of the Supreme Soviet in Moscow. The same was true for all industrial production — planned high up in the government in Moscow, far away from the actual fabrication. What a bureaucratic waste!

The official orders were: Every manufacturing plant will run at full speed. Machines will last forever and never break down. Supplies from other places will always arrive on time and railroad cars for shipment will always be available. Everything will run under perfect conditions. The production figures are always right because the bureaucrats expect them to be so. Every lower Soviet official or director of a factory or party boss is concerned about keeping his lucrative position and privileges. They find ways to "fulfill" the five-year plan, and may even receive a medal, a bonus, or a promotion if everything in the reports to Moscow is according to plan and above.

The system didn't really work. It was all on paper — the plan, the production, the harvest, and the reports. No one had the courage to admit it was a sham. It was a sacred cow. The boat must not be rocked. This system had to eventually come to a grinding halt and collapse. Two years after the war, every shortage was blamed on World War II and promises were made that everything would be available soon. The people were kept in a state of promises forever.

Doomed to Rot In the wagon factory, the names of the best workers and their percentage of overproduction were written on a big blackboard. Things like that were required in the "worker's paradise," where everyone did his best for the well-being of the Soviet Socialistic Society.

One day I had to accompany the engineer in his search for a part they needed to repair one of the turning lathes. The German engineer and I walked outside the plant behind the last inspection station that led to the main railroad track. Along the way we saw parts of railroad cars that had fallen off as they were pulled out of the plant after final inspection. They had been counted in the production quota but were not usable for transportation.

We found some rare original machines, well crated for shipment. They were lying on both sides of the track where they had been dumped from a railroad car. Some crates had been opened and the contents exposed to the wind and weather. Those machines had come from German factories, been shipped all over the Soviet Union, and then left to rust in the outdoors. We found a part that we needed for the lathe, but wondered who was well trained enough to remove it without damaging it. There was so much need and so much waste; nothing seemed to harmonize and work together for good.

Moral Armament My men worked in many different departments, so I had to walk quite a few kilometers in a day. I looked after the four-hour workers, too, and saw that they were not put to heavy labor. They sometimes had to be encouraged to perform their assigned work. Like everywhere else in the world, there were men who did not mind working. They did their jobs as well as possible. And there were others who sat on their butts every chance they got and complained about everything: too cold, too hot, not enough to eat, not enough clothing; we should be sent home. Those guys could create problems and needed diplomatic persuasion to smooth out their moods before they got out of hand. Sometimes I advised them to get tough, get out of their rotten moods, and overcome their self-pity.

"You are not the only ones suffering, "I told them." We are all in the same boat, so make the best of it."

It made no difference what those guys said about me. They saw me walking around, not "working," and did not understand why I asked them to do what I apparently didn't do myself. I did my best to keep things running smoothly and saw to it that every man was fairly evaluated for the work he performed. Unfortunately, the four-hour workers had no chance to earn rubles. They could not even get supplemental bread for work well done. I couldn't blame them for their thoughts — it was the fault of the system. It recognized only the ones who made the norm or more, which was only possible for eight-hour workers. But the weaker men, who were more in need of additional bread and food to get back on their feet, were denied. The funny thing was that the Soviets in charge, who denied God and the Bible, quoted both at every occasion:

"If any would not work, neither shall he eat." (II Thessalonians 3:10 KJV) They said the same, only in a short version:

"No work, no bread."

Music in the Camp I had compassion for those four-hour workers. I understood their feelings, but for their own sake I tried to pull them out of their brooding. Maybe they hated me for that. Two years before, I was glad to be on a job working outside the camp. Now I was glad to be back in camp and away from problems at the factory. Yes, it was good to be in the camp. It had changed so much during the past year. We had a committee of WPs to look after our mental well-being. They even arranged some entertainment, and the performers were anyone who had anything to offer. It was a simple talent show. The Russians "organized" instruments, and we got together a band: a violin, a saxophone, an accordion, and percussion instruments. If they had a chance to practice, the music sounded pretty good. But for special requests, the music did not sound so well. On Sundays, at the noon meal, we held a concert in the dining hall. It was very well received.

Our entertainment program coordinator Otto Fuhlbruegge and I became good friends. He was from Dortmund, where my parents lived for a while. He wanted to know what we could do with our limited resources. In the modest library, we now had German and Russian books written in German. I found a book of German poetry, and in it was a poem by Matthias Claudius, "*Der Mond ist aufgegagen*" (The Moon Is Risen). This poem was set to music and expressed my philosophy. It begins:

"The moon is risen and shines. The silver stars are shining in the sky so clear and bright.... Do you see the moon up there? Only half is to be seen, but yet it is round and beautiful. So it is with many things we laugh at because our eyes cannot see them clearly." Claudius wrote the poem in 1779. His poetry expresses great insight. It was what I felt inside.

Camp Production Three of us worked together: Otto, Hermann Krauss and I. Hermann was a schoolteacher from Gueglingen in Wuertemberg. Besides being a teacher, he was an organist in the local church and a philosopher in his way. We exchanged thoughts from our different backgrounds and did not always agree. We spent many evenings together just talking. We did not talk about our conditions, our surroundings, or our lack of "things." Rather, it was a conversation about literature, music, our home country, and what life had allowed us to experience.

Hermann was with Group III and had to work only four hours. He was small of stature. When he was occasionally assigned to my brigade, he did as well as he could on any job. And if he did not have enough strength, he looked at me with a twinkle in his eyes as if to say, "I did my best. That is all I have to give."

He was never down — always content with what he had. I learned this truth: When a man knows who he is, he's content with whatever he has.

We put the program together and it went well. Our orchestra practiced long and hard. We sang some songs — not army songs, but folk songs from different parts of Germany. Hermann read stories about different areas in Germany. Ending up, we heard Claudius' words in the last verse, which were so fitting:

"So lay down my brethren, in the name of God, cold is the evening breeze. God protect us from evil, and give us a quiet night, and to our ill neighbors too."

I had no voice to sing those beautiful words. If one is not familiar with the text in a song, the words and their meanings often get lost. It is important to listen to what the words are trying to express. We decided to let our orchestra play the melody very softly, and I would speak the text slowly so the words would be understood. When I spoke those words from Matthias Claudius, not one pair of eyes stayed dry. They expressed our deepest thoughts.

Winter Comes When winter arrived, we were issued more substantial uniforms and even fur caps. And how we needed them! Our camp was on the edge of the prairie and exposed to the wind from whatever direction it blew — in the morning from the east and at night it came back blowing from the west. It was a barren landscape — no trees, no bushes to hold back the wind. Someone had known these conditions when they built the "barracks" halfway underground with small windows at ground level. The good earth was a better insulation than the sawdust in the walls of the sawmill camp. There were no bedbugs here, and even the body lice population was less since we showered at least twice a week with really hot water in a bathhouse right inside the camp. The snow blew over the earth bunkers, and only when it accumulated too much did we have to shovel it from the windows to let in a little light. It did not make much difference since the lightbulbs were lit day and night. I don't think the light switch was yet invented in Russia. Electricity was wired directly into the light socket. Why would you want to turn off the light? Be proud and show you have electricity in your Russian house. Let it always shine!

With the change to winter clothing, the brigadiers received sheepskin coats — not like women in Europe wear with fur for show on the outside, but with the fur on the inside. I loved my coat. Not only was it warm and good protection against the wind, but it was tailored with a flared bottom so it was comfortable to move and walk in.

St. Nick's Warm-Up On an early December day, when it had snowed for weeks, the wind was chasing the snowflakes in one direction, then another, as if the flakes were trying to play catch. Coming out of the dining hall, one hurried to make it back to his underground hut. There were days we wore our coats to the dining hall so the soup in our bellies would not freeze on the way back. A piece of free-hanging railroad rail that someone beat on was our signal to get up in the morning for the meals and to go to work. The sound carried far. The person who was in charge must have enjoyed the job since he did not seem to want to stop this time.

We joked, "Air raid? The Americans are coming?"

Then someone stepped outside and saw that the bunker across from ours was on fire. It was the storage hut for all our clothes and shoes. It was in full blaze. Some of our men fought the fire to no avail. The flames shot out of an opening at the top that had burned through. The new and old clothes fed the flames. The fire truck from the factory came, but it was almost too late. The men were well trained. They carried their own water, laid out the hose and in no time had water pouring on the flames. It took them quite awhile to extinguish the fire. It smoldered for days.

The guys who had turned in their pants or jackets for repair had it the worst. We had a WP tailor who repaired our uniforms, so we looked fairly decent — much better than during our first year in the sawmill camp. It happened on the evening of December 6, 1947, the German St. Nicholas Day.

Blackboards The fourth brigade ran smoothly. I had learned all of the tricks in bookkeeping, fighting for the *naryads*, spending long hours in the evenings tallying everything on paper, and turning the documents in on time.

An electrician in my brigade installed an electrical line and socket right beside my bed so I could do my paperwork at night without bothering those around me who wanted to sleep. The bunk was my "office"—chair to sit in with knees for a desk.

In the rear of our bunker was a room where sixteen men slept. My lower bunk was close to the small window. I kept the office supplies—ink, pen, and a little paper—well hidden inside my straw sack. In order to go outside, we had to walk through the main sleeping room of about 120 men. It was amazing how warm it was inside the bunker. We were protected from the wind, insulated by the earth, and at night warmed by our body heat and gas from some individuals. The air was thick and stale by morning, however.

There were two large blackboards in the dining hall. One had the menu for the day and the calories we would receive. It was written very impressively, but we knew better. We would get weak soups and kasha. Every person with an official or unofficial function in the camp helped himself to the food supply: a little sugar, a little oil, a little piece of meat, half a loaf of bread, some flour, millet grits, or whatever else was available. Just a little here and a little there, but there were so many—WPs doing extra chores and helping in the kitchen, and the man keeping the bathhouse clean. All those got a little more to eat. It reduced our calorie supply substantially. If we always had received the correct ration as scheduled, there would be no Group III or dystrophic men. It was not only a limited amount, but the nourishment was usually starches, not much protein, and no fresh fruit or vegetables other than the cabbage and green tomatoes floating in our soup once in a while.

The other blackboard charted the monthly percentage of individual brigades. The brigades that had only Group III men with four-hour shifts could never reach the quota required. There was no comparison to my fourth brigade with all the eight-hour workers. We were always the best brigade, with over 100 percent. The system was not fair. I was lucky to be assigned to a brigade with so many specialists that caused the percentages to come out so high. But still I had to be on the ball to get the *naryads* in correctly and on time. I would be surprised if the *natchalniks* ever wrote the honest amount for the four-hour workers.

Christmas Christmas was just around the corner. Otto Fuhlbruegge, Hermann Krauss, and I planned a Christmas party with a special dinner. The kitchen would withhold a small part of the rations so a larger portion could be served on Christmas Day. Just this one time we wanted to have a special occasion. The Russian commandant did not go for the idea. Maybe he knew his people. If the cook withheld a little every day there would be more in storage for the "officials" to carry out. We were disappointed and wondered how we would celebrate Christmas—maybe coming together for some Christmas songs. "*Nyet.*" That is a German tradition. We celebrated Father Frost on December 21, and that was it. No holiday dinner, nothing.

The day before Christmas, as I came in with my brigade, the guard opened the gate and counted the men. The number had to be the same when we came in as when we went out. I was about to follow the last man when he stopped me, went into the guardhouse, and came back out with a five-foot branch from a fir tree. Someone had brought it for the WPs. I was so surprised I stuttered.

"*Spasibo.*" ("Thank you.") I took that branch and told Otto about it. We decided to hang it high in the dining room so everybody could see it. I asked my electrician to string a wire for a bulb so we could have at least one light on our Christmas branch. Since there were no switches, it would shine at all times for a couple of days. By Christmas morning, for the breakfast meal, the bulb was gone. Someone had found a better use for it, I guess. The whole camp enjoyed the Christmas branch. But it hung on the wall as if it was crucified, rather than symbolizing the joy of Jesus' birth. It was not the food, the light, or the branch that was meaningful — but the reality that *in the fullness of time* Christ was born.

The few of us who knew how the branch had come into the camp wondered about the person who was acquainted with the German customs and tried to share with us our Christmas tradition. Was it someone from the factory, or someone from Engels? We never found out, but it touched us deeply that some Russian cared.

The Restroom As the brigadier and leader of the best brigade in the factory, I enjoyed some privileges. I could walk through the front gate of the factory at any time and visit the little bazaar. On warmer days and before fall came, one *babushka*, the grandmother-type Russian, regularly sold homemade bread, milk, cheese, and sometimes *piroshkis*. When I met her for the first time, I was surprised that she spoke German — kind of a low German. She never said very much, and it was always indirect.

"When you WPs go home, then our husbands and sons will come back."

That was her hope. On earlier visits with her, I found out that during the war men and families with German names from Engels and Marx (the Volga-German colonies) were taken away. Where to? She did not know, and they were never heard from again. I could tell she had told me more than she wanted to. On later visits, she did not mention the subject again. And I did not ask questions. One never knew who was listening.

The two red brick buildings on either side of the factory gate looked quite attractive.

The building to the left was the cafeteria and store where employees could buy groceries — if there was something for sale. To the right was a two-story administration building with big windows, almost European style. It housed the accounting offices, the engineering department, and the factory director and his staff. The engineer and draftsman from my brigade worked there, so I had the right to go into the building. This building was always warm with steam heat fired by natural gas. It was built shortly before the war, I'd guess, and was almost elegant compared to the dirt floors and negligent appearance of the factory halls.

On one of those visits, one of the Russian engineers said my two men were good workers — they knew how to fix things and were a big help in keeping production moving. As I was visiting with my men, a secretary from another department walked toward the end of the building away from the gate. I asked the men where she was going — probably to the outhouse, they said. Toilets had been forgotten in the planning of the building. There was a piece of gossip: The director had a commode. Everybody else had to parade by the windows on the first floor so everyone would know they were going to the outhouse. Gerd, the engineer, said, "Hansarmin, go out there and take a look."

Approximately one hundred feet from the administration building, there was a shed divided into two sections by a wood partition. Half of the wooden floor was raised about eight inches with two holes in it. It was winter and people's leavings were frozen solid. No one must have serviced this building in winter, feeling that spring would take care of matters. I assumed they depended on the honey wagon system I remembered so well from sawmill camp days. I never went back.

The Conference

Walking on Water A wonderful rumor spread through the camp—in Saratov there would be a conference for the whole district to honor the best workers and those in charge. There would be an overnight stay at a special camp, with speeches, toasts, and recognition of the best men, the best brigade, and the best everything. Our camp would be represented. The head brigadier, Willi, would go, Otto Fuhlbruegge, the event coordinator, some of the best workers in my brigade, and I would go as brigadier of one of the best brigades in the district. What an experience! Willi thought I should give a speech, but I told him, "No way. I'd rather stay home."

He said he would do it for me. Otto told me details of the event. We would walk across the frozen Volga, by far the shortest route.

The day came for the event, which meant I would be out of the factory for a full two days. There were six of us, and we walked through the gate without a guard. We were allowed to leave by ourselves!

We went toward Engels. The Volga was white, glittering, covered with snow and frozen solid. I was amazed we could walk on it.

Hundreds of people were coming and going. They crossed with sleds and trucks. It was a sunny, cold day, and everyone we saw was in a good mood. People meeting friends greeted and hugged. Some had bottles under their coats and passed drinks around. It was like a carnival, a people's fete. I walked like I was on cloud nine. I don't think the people around us noticed we were WPs. I wore my fur coat and fur cap and did not look much different than some of the Russians, except for my shoes. Most of the Russians walked in high, heavy felt boots to keep their feet warm.

I never saw Russians so happy. Was it the sunny day crossing the Volga? Were they going visiting, shopping, or just to the other side? They walked in both directions. Some walked briskly and steadily, not seeing anything. Others strolled and seemed to enjoy the walk across the river. I talked to myself to make sure it was real, that I was allowed to do what I was doing—walking across the Volga! It must be frozen deep down since horse-drawn sleds and trucks crossed. I knew the waters of the Volga kept running even if the top was frozen solid. I

The Volga was frozen solid. Hundreds of people were coming and going.

walked the "waters" of the Volga! From the days in the sawmill camp, when I sat on the stairs leading to the upper room, looking out at the Volga, my meditation came back to me!

Drop by drop they joined together from melting snow, raindrops falling from the sky, one drop coming into the other, running to the riverbed by the law of gravity — sometimes flowing slowly, sometimes faster in the narrows, but always on the move. And now the little drops stood still for a while, packed tightly together to allow happy people to cross from shore to shore, then melting again, the cycle of all things, ultimately to return to whence they came.

How far away those days in the sawmill camp seemed to be. I assumed people hoped things would get better. The war was won. They had gone through real suffering; now a turn for the better should come. Instead came a rumor, or was it propaganda? Was it meant to scare the people again? Was it to keep the people in line?

"*Vojeno budit.*" ("There will be war again!") The civilian who told us was very serious. America had occupied Iran, and the American Air Force had taken over the airfields in that country.

Some of us daydreamed about whether the Americans came from the south, and if so, might they not come along the river? The Russians may yet shoot us or deport us to Siberia or someplace to the east — maybe we would all be lost and nobody would ever know. The country is so big even people close by would not know something or someone was hidden there. The country stretches over two continents — part Europe and endless Asia to the Pacific, from the Kara Sea in the North to the Black Sea in the South. It covers eleven time zones.

I was so taken with my thoughts I did not notice how quickly we reached the other side of the river. Up the embankment, we came to the first houses. In an open square a little to our right stood an Orthodox church. It looked neglected, but not like some others used for storage or machine shops with discarded parts and debris lying around. I had an urge to go inside and told the others:

"I want to just take a glimpse of what is inside. Walk a bit slower and I will catch up."

Moment of Silence I walked up, opened the door, and took my fur cap off as I entered the church. I knew there would be no pews or benches inside, but there were a few people. They seemed not to notice me. I stood in silence and said not even a formal prayer. Being there with those Russian believers was enough, even if we could not communicate with each other; just to know there were others who knew there was a living God Almighty, Creator of Heaven and Earth. A God over war and peace, over tragedy and joy, sorrow and laughter. Alleluia, for the Lord God omnipotent reigneth. There was a tie that bound us together, yet we exchanged no words. I was only in the church for about a minute.

My thoughts took me back to the Cathedral of Riga during the war. It was Easter Sunday. I had gone there just to see what was going on. Inside, German soldiers mingled with civilians listening to the singing between the Bishop with the miter standing beneath the altar and the choir of male voices responding from the balcony across. I did not understand the words — was it Greek or Latvian? But at the high point someone said in German:

"The Lord is risen."

"He is risen indeed!" was the response, and with those words the people embraced. It was not the language, but the knowing behind the words. The flashback went quickly. I hurried to catch up with my companions. They did not ask and I did not volunteer anything.

Otto suggested that we take the *elektrishka* (streetcar). It was the end stop, and most of the passengers came from across the Volga. Otto paid for the six of us. The conductor asked me something I did not understand. I answered "*Da, Da,*" and he turned to the next passenger. It felt like one big family there in the streetcar. But then, aren't we one big family despite race, color, or language?

The Lucky Ones Somewhere we had to get off the *elektrishka*. Otto was leading like a local citizen. It was not a long walk to the camp where the best worker conference would be held. What would it be? Propaganda with banners, slogans that we are here to build up what Germans had destroyed, slogans to encourage the comrades to produce more and better, and if we go home some day, we should tell the world what a great nation the Union of Soviet Socialist Republics is — her strength, her glory, the paradise for the working class of Russia. I was so sick and tired of that propaganda.

The program was ready to begin. We registered and got a name tag in both German and Russian, stating what camp we were from. We were categorized and put in our pigeonholes, so to speak. Willi was waiting for us when we arrived. He was a handsome fellow: tall, black hair, with eyes that sparkled. When he smiled one had to respond. He always knew a way out of any problem, and had an answer for every situation.

"I missed you this morning when we left, Willi. How did you get here?"

"I had to leave the night before to prepare for this important conference."

He had hopped on one of those trucks and passed us on the way over the Volga. I got the picture. He had spent the night with that good-looking blonde girl from one of the administration offices. Now I knew why Willi was often so knowledgeable about what was going on in the factory. He always kept me well informed too. Our eyes met. We both understood, and nothing more was said.

The best workers came from a wide area around Saratov, and we felt awkward being advertised as the elite. We knew many others worked hard, too, and maybe harder than us "best workers." Who says life is fair? There will always be haves and have-nots. The only thing I'd like to see change is for the haves not to think they are better than the have-nots. A rumor circulated around the camp that there would be a surprise that evening. Our group would stay overnight because of the distance from Engels. The evening meal was later than normal. In the dining room, we took our seats at the white paper-covered tables, with fork and spoon at every place. (Prisoners always carried their own spoons for soup and *kasha*.) We could not believe our eyes. We were to be served right at the table! It was embarrassing because the servers were prisoners just like us. They didn't seem to mind and were amused by our expressions of surprise. I figured they would get a second helping from the leftovers. The soup was a stew we could have eaten with a fork. Then came potato *kasha*. This was solid mashed potatoes, prepared with oil and very tasty. Instead of the usual slice of bread, they brought us a piece of cheesecake.

We were well fed, willing to listen to speeches and slogans.

Like an important banquet, the head table was reserved for Russian and German camp commanders. One of the higher-ranking Russian officers spoke and someone translated. He welcomed us and explained we were being honored because of our good work and production; every camp represented here had pitched in to make this event possible.

The Conference

Almost three years had passed since the war ended. Many former German soldiers had done their best to make up for what they had been ordered to destroy. The Russian officer did not push for more production, rather he looked back at what had been accomplished. That officer won our hearts. He understood how we felt. He did not mention the word WP. We were all surprised, as we never expected anything like that. Then came the calling of names for the best workers. There were many with higher percentages than our men for individual production. Then came the best brigadiers. For the past three months, brigade four from the wagon factory in Engels had been the best. There was applause. I was expected to stand up and give a speech. I had already told Willi I wouldn't give a talk.

I pointed to Willi, indicating he should speak for me. He started out by saying I was too shy to stand up before so large a crowd, and so on. After he finished, there was more applause and I got up. I said nothing, but I thought, if they only knew.

He knew what I had done. He taught me how every man in the brigade could be paid in rubles. Some men made more money than they could be paid according to the rules — 400 rubles to the camp. That was for room and board, then 85 percent of up to 150 rubles could be paid out. Anything above that amount was lost. But I transferred those wages to other men who had not done quite as well because of their type of work. I spent a lot of time calculating amounts so nothing would be wasted, and every man in the brigade would get some rubles. The specialty workers always got their full pay, and the others "earned" some of the overrun. It worked and had little to do with the fourth brigade being the best.

More speeches, more applause, then came the best part of the event — we got acquainted with WPs from other camps and heard their stories. It was good to hear about other places. We were not doing so bad after all in our camp at Engels: the factory and the working conditions. We had a wonderful time, and were served that delicious evening meal. What would come next? The speaker's podium was moved. They set up music stands for an orchestra, and it looked like it would be more of a real orchestra than the one we had in Engels. This must be the surprise they talked about earlier in the afternoon. And it was. The men of this camp had put together the musical, *Das Weisse Roessl* (*The White Horse Inn*). It was unbelievable — a perfect stage set, full orchestra, and costumes. The women's roles were played and sung by male WPs. Their voices were a bit lower than in the original play, but what a delight! The music alone was worth the entire effort of our attending.

Slow Return We spent the night and ate the usual morning meal. The next day it was back to normal again. We had a full day ahead of us returning to our camp. Otto had explored possibilities and made plans for us to do something out of the ordinary on the way home. We would walk into town and mingle with the pedestrians. We noticed most of the people walked singly. Very seldom did two walk together. We were a herd of six, which was a traffic stopper, so we split up and fit in just fine.

We went to a *sennaja* (department store) like GUM in Moscow, only much smaller and with hardly any merchandise on display. People were standing in line everywhere. If there was a shelf stocked with merchandise, people waited in line to buy whatever it was. There were hardly any salespeople to serve the shoppers. The triple lines, one next to the other, were a puzzle at first — one line to choose, if there was a choice (mostly there was only one item for sale), a second line to pay for what one bought, and a third line for wrapping the merchandise, if there was enough newspaper. What impressed me most was that the people in the line just stood there. Very few talked to each other, and the younger ones had something to read. The lines had both old and young: some military officers, but mostly the *babushkas*, the Russian grandmothers who did the shopping for the whole family. Looking around, I noticed there was no line at the foot-operated sewing machines. Since nobody else was around, I took a closer look at them. The cast iron, ornamental sides were so rough with burrs one could easily get cut just by moving the sewing machine, and the price was over six hundred rubles, more than the average worker's monthly wage. Nobody seemed to notice us, even though we spoke German to each other.

We must have appeared not too different from the Russians as we strolled the street back to the Volga crossing. No one paid any attention to us. Otto and I with our "elegant" fur coats and fur caps looked well dressed compared to the average citizen, as long as no one looked at our shoes. It was enjoyable strolling through the streets, not hurrying and with no obligations — nothing to do but watch the people. Many walked at a good pace. The older ones moved more slowly.

Fast-Food Service We stopped at a street vendor for a *piroshki*, a pastry filled with cabbage and sometimes with cottage cheese. I remembered *piroshkis* filled with deliciously prepared meat, but that was ten years ago in a Russian restaurant in Berlin. Here in Russia we had street corner service — the food not piping hot, but fresh. We decided not to form a line of six, but to have Otto buy them for us. His Russian was the best. He could not hold all of the *piroshkis*, and there was no paper to wrap them in. Despite our careful planning, we had to crowd around the stand and made some commotion while each of us got our *piroshki*.

We arrived at the Volga fairly early in the afternoon and began our walk back to Engels. There were not as many people along the way as there had been the morning before. We talked about our experiences, the food, the *White Horse Inn* play, and the men we met from other camps, as well as their working conditions. It had been quite an education. The crossing went fast. We were "home" just in time for the evening soup. It was good to be back in my own bunk. As I pondered all these things, I was content with my situation compared with what we had heard and seen.

There and Here

Mystery News An old East Berlin newspaper in the library did not make much sense. That Germany was divided into four zones was understandable. But Berlin divided into four sectors: American, British, French, and Russian? I could not picture how that could be.

Besides the Berlin newspaper, there were some books of Russian literature printed in German. One statement from a book by Pushkin stuck in my mind: "Nowhere does time pass so fast as in Russia, except in prison."

Yes, time did go fast, and the real blessing was we had work to do. The more insight I got into the Communist system, the more I knew it could not work forever. I could not speak with authority about Moscow, Kiev, or Leningrad. Those cities are not representative of the whole nation, but showcases for the world. The people out in the country, the mass of workers, are the nation. They are slaves of this system, condemned to destruction. Russia has so much potential: the vast farmlands, the treasure of her soil and minerals. I made a strong statement to Otto:

"I am not afraid of Communism, for this system will surely fail. It is thirty years after the revolution, and living conditions are still under par. The workers' paradise exists only in phrases, slogans, and propaganda."

The shortage of goods was always blamed on the war. Russia suffered greatly during the war, losing millions of its citizens. People had to sacrifice everything for the great war. But even three years after the victory, the conditions had not improved. If Russia could produce like a free enterprise country, Communism could be a threat to the world. But the irony is, if they developed a free enterprise system contrary to Communist theory, Communism would no longer be. What are thirty years or fifty or one hundred years to world history? The Supreme Soviet would not admit their failure and go in another direction that would be against all principles and "accomplishments" of the 1917 revolution.

What had happened to Germany — total destruction — could bring about the necessary change. With the destruction, we were free from the Nazis. If that happened to Russia, a complete collapse of the economy, they could abandon the centrally planned and dictated system. Hitler and Stalin, to keep their dictatorial

In the high grass surrounding the factory, Misha and I could talk and not be seen.

systems going, were not so far apart when they made an agreement not to attack each other. How long did it last — until Hitler's attack on Russia? Surprise? Neither one of them trusted the other!

Compassion The civilians we worked with had understanding and compassion for the WPs. We had teams of Russian workers and WPs on a machine or oven and they became well acquainted. If a WP helper was sick, the Russians were concerned and expressed hope it was not serious. Many did not see us only as WPs, but as human beings. They seemed to know what it meant to be a prisoner. I do not exaggerate when I say every Russian family has someone who is in the *zaklyuchony*—the civilian labor camp. Yes, they knew what it was to miss a loved one.

Spring 1948 came and there were hardly any flowers. The warm winds blew and took the snow cover. The ground dried out and turned the muddy roads into solid ground. The sun not only lengthened the light of our days, but it sent rays to warm our hearts and bodies.

Misha A new face showed up in the plant: a young man in his late twenties, maybe twenty-eight, always dressed in an officer's army coat with no insignia. He walked in a dashing fashion. We met through a work assignment. As I spoke in my broken Russian, he answered in German only slightly better than my Russian. We both laughed at our attempt to communicate. He already knew my name and told me his name was Misha. Misha had a boyish, free look about him. The blonde hair of his youth had begun to darken a little. His blue eyes were always on the move like they were searching for the unknown, the unseen. With his predominant cheekbones, he was to me the typical Russian. We became friendly. He invited me to march out into the high grass surrounding the factory where we could talk and not be seen. He was uncomplicated, open, and as we talked we discovered that we had much in common.

Misha had been a lieutenant during the war and was now assigned to the wagon factory as a kind of overseer. He wore his army coat, he confessed, because it was the only one he had. He was married and had a little girl. We usually met late morning or early afternoon in the meadow and called it *"Auf der Wiese."* He liked that expression. He had taught himself German, but was eager to converse and learn to pronounce better. Misha was a very good student. The Russians seem to be gifted in learning languages. Misha wanted to know all about my life, my family; what I had done before the war. As I spoke slowly to him, he closed his eyes to concentrate on my words. Whenever he spoke back to me in German he wanted to be corrected. Then he would repeat and repeat until he got the meaning and the proper pronunciation. It was fun being together. The next day Misha would speak correctly — or almost correctly — the German words he had learned the previous day.

Our conversation was mostly about conditions in the USSR — the shortcomings, the economy, and so on. He showed me clearly that the Soviet was not Russia, and Russia was not the Soviet. It confirmed my own observations. The system is one thing, then there were the land and the Russian people.

I told Misha when I returned home I would emigrate to the United States. He seemed to envy me and said what a lucky fellow I was to have such a great future. He begged me to tell people wherever I went: "The Russian people need help from the outside. We want no more war. War does not solve problems; it only makes things worse. What is needed is a political leader who will stand against Stalin and his government."

I told him Stalin could not live forever and a change in leadership would bring a new political direction. He pointed out again and again that pressure from the outside was necessary. He knew well the situation his country was in.

We developed a very close friendship and respected each other as equals. I did not talk about him in camp. Whenever we met inside the factory, we both acted very official. But the twinkle in his eyes said, "Let us meet *Auf der Wiese.*"

The Fence

The Preparation With the coming of spring, a plan developed for a great project. The plant engineer was excited about an order to build an iron fence that would enclose a park in front of the main entrance to the factory. What park? In soil where nothing grew except weeds? "*Park budit.*" There will be a park with trees, bushes, and benches for the workers.

The engineer was a short, slender fellow, with short black hair. He walked briskly, always on the move. His black eyes were piercing, and he always worked against time, expecting the impossible. He seemed not to trust anyone. Listening to our conversation, one would think we were from different planets — I in my Russian and German intermixed and he in his Russian and a little German that sounded more like Yiddish — but we communicated, and that was all that was important. When he left, a woman working at the oven close by made a gesture putting a folded finger to her nose, enlarging the looks of it. He always call me Brigadier, never by my name. He said I should organize the men for welding the fence and moving the sections to their locations in front of the plant. It had to be accomplished without interruption of the main production. I assume the engineer had confidence I would be able to handle the project, so I tried to do the best under the given conditions and discussed any problem with him. It was decided that the fence would be built from one-inch metal straps cut to precise lengths and welded together. My welder wanted to know how much money he would get before he started. He wanted to be paid by the piece, not by the hour. I suggested to the engineer that we would have to design a jig to get a uniform pattern and for faster welding.

"Good thought, go ahead, make a jig."

"But it needs to be designed and the material for the jig should not be scrap."

The jig had to be built sturdy to be used many times over.

"Okay, okay, you will get the material."

"But who will pay for the time to make the drawings and build the jig?"

"*Vojeno pleny, nix good.*"

We had learned to nail everything down to the smallest detail and even then it was difficult to get paid for what had already been agreed upon. I made very slow progress in the preparation.

When we made the jigs — one for the fence section and one for the columns — we had problems getting the straps to lay out so we could go to work. With every day's delay the engineer got more noticeably nervous. I wondered if Stalin was coming in person to inspect the plant. Did the fence have to be in place to impress him? Pressure to get the project completed was intense.

The real problem was that the shear crew did not want to cut the straps. They cut side panels for freight cars — big four-by-six foot sheets of steel — and were paid by the pound. No wonder their names were on the best-worker's blackboard every month. It was heavy work and the weight gave them the production overrun. When I asked them to cut one-inch straps to a precise length, they laughed. They would have to work all day just to get the same weight they ordinarily did in an hour or two.

The welder who was to do the job threatened to quit. If he could not work the way he wanted to, he'd look for another job. He wanted the rubles due him at the end of the month. I was caught in the middle between the engineer, his men, and my own men. What happened next was a miracle. The next morning, the first bundle of straps had been cut and was lying by the shear. I assumed the night shift had done it. I organized their move to the forge where there was room for our assembly line. We worked out some of the kinks and by noon break had the first few fence panels piled up. We discovered that Paul, the welder, could not work continuously. While taking the finished fence off and putting the new straps into the jig, he had to wait. We decided to build a second jig — one to weld and the other to prepare the layout. It was not too difficult to locate usable material, and we did it on our own time. With this second jig completed, we could go into real production. The four-hour morning and afternoon shift workers laid the straps in one jig while the welder worked on the other one. They removed the finished panel from the first jig and prepared it with straps so Paul could weld without stopping. We had a continuous work flow going. Even the men from the shorter shifts enjoyed working together on this efficient production line. It was my job to make certain we always had enough straps cut so our assembly line would not be slowed by a shortage of material. The workers on the shear always cussed me, but I was used to that; the only important thing was that we accomplished our assignment. One day when the engineer rushed by, seeing the fence sections piling up, he praised us:

"*Gute organisatoren!*" ("Good organizers!")

We took it as a compliment.

A Commission I looked forward to my times with Misha. We respected and trusted each other. On one of our many talks, I told him:

"Misha, I hope you understand what I am about to say. I feel free in this prisoners' camp. We will go home someday. We will not be here forever. But you and your people must remain in this land. You are the ones who are really fenced in. I am not able to share my thoughts, because few would understand."

I mentioned my experience in the hospital at Atkarsk where I was not free. I was in bondage. I told Misha how I had not eaten more than everyone else in hopes of being sickly enough to go home. I was under the obsession I could force my return home; that last day, I was called back as the others left to go home. I was the only one called back. After the storm inside me settled, I asked myself, How did this happen? A still, small voice came to me and although it did not answer my question, it gave me this promise:

"In the fullness of time, you will go home. No matter what condition you are in."

I knew the promise came from God, the same God I thanked before and after every meal, no matter how little food there was. I thought I had faith before, but for sure I had it now. I had an encounter with God.

I spoke very slowly, and Misha repeated every word I said so gently. He was understanding. It felt good when he interrupted:

"Hansarmin, I know you will go home."

There was a sadness in his voice. He knew I would go home, but he had to stay. He beseeched me to tell everybody what I had heard and seen here—*tell them* the Russian people need help from the outside.

"We have a different language, different culture, but the one thing we have in common is our longing for 'freedom.'"

We shook hands, Misha and I, in a silent pact that expressed more than any words could ever have said.

Sounds Early summer came. The nights were fair and warm, and it was pleasant to be outdoors. It was toward the end of the month, and I had to work late to finish my bookkeeping for the brigade. The men around me were all sound asleep. I looked my sheets over one last time to be sure my figures were correct. I had an urge to get some fresh air. The air inside got heavy, especially if it was contaminated. All kinds of odors came at you—body odors such as gas, feet, smoke. It was there and it was strong.

In order to get outside it was necessary to go through the larger room. Someone was always up and smoking in the room. The tiny glow of a cigarette could be seen. When I got out, I took in a deep breath of the fresh night air and then another one, and another. I was lifted up and felt so elevated I almost fainted. What silence—no snoring, no groaning. Even the guards in their watchtowers were quiet. Almost too quiet. Maybe one of them was asleep, or maybe not even at his lookout. Sometimes, especially at night, they could be heard singing or just humming a melody. They did not sing army songs, but melodies from their home region. I'll bet they were as homesick as we were. I sat down and breathed normally, allowing the quietness of the night to come upon me. There was a faint tone in the silence. It was like the sound of humming in the air. I had to concentrate to hear that sound of silence. I could feel something in the air. Even though my wife and son were a long way off, I was not alone. I could not explain it. It was one of those things that each person has to experience for himself:

"*So ist's mit manchen Sachen, die wir getrost belachen, weil unsere Augen sie nicht seh'n*" (Matthias Claudias). ("So it is with many things we try to laugh off, because our eyes cannot see them.")

I returned to my bunk, passing through the heavy air, breathing very lightly so as not to disturb the fresh air deep in my lungs. I laid down and I was filled with peace. I had experienced a new thing I had not known existed: How beautiful a night's sleep could be when you were in harmony with the Almighty!

Happiness Is How You Look at Things After the morning routine, everyone went to their job assignments. The girls were in an unusually happy mood. Some were giggling and laughing. It did not take too long before some of them had to tell us what was up. They lifted their long pants or their skirts a little and showed us very proudly their new stockings — all the same color. Those girls were so happy to have some new woolen — or were they heavy cotton — stockings? We too laughed with the girls because we had never seen a color like that in stockings — an odd lilac-blue-violet. It was a mishmash that could never have sold in the big city. They had to be shipped to the countryside, where they made somebody happy.

An Argument It was late, toward quitting time. I was arguing with one of the *natchalniks* about some *naryads* that did not show the correct percentages and amounts of rubles due the men. The brigade was already assembled and waiting for me. The brigadier should be the first one in line, not the last. Before I left, I told the *natchalnik* he would get no men tomorrow to do his work until the *naryads* were corrected. I was steaming! Here I was trying to get the correct documents and had sixty men waiting for me. Finally, I succeeded. As I approached the waiting men I could feel the tension in the air from the men and from the guards. One of the guards came at me with gun in hand. He said I was a son of something, cursed, and started to lower the shaft of his rifle on me. I had a flashback to the time I was beaten on the trip to Breslau because I tried to enlarge the hole in the boxcar. As that pain came back to me, I stepped right up close to the soldier, looked him right in the eyes, and said in my broken Russian:

"I had to argue with a *natchalnik* about the documents for the work completed. Your rotten system allows you to cheat the WPs whenever possible."

He brought his gun down and stepped back, but I moved closer, face to face. I almost stepped on his toes. The whole scene must have appeared funny. I could hear somebody snickering behind me and somebody else said in German, very fast, "Don't laugh, this is serious!"

The guard gave in and told me to get in line. We marched to the gate, and the gate guard counted the men with me at his side. Not one word was exchanged. I had learned to stand up to them. They respected authority. If I had ducked, the guard would have beaten me up. That I remembered all too well.

Rumors It was summer. Everything in the camp and at the factory was running normally. The fence production was going well. The pressure to produce more was always there, but not as intense as it was at the beginning of the project. A rumor was circulating that the four-hour workers Group III, would be pulled out of the camp. We knew the full-time laborers could not handle what was demanded of us at the wagon factory. By now, it was very clear how much we needed those four-hour workers, and how well they fit into the production when properly organized. When I first heard about Group III, I didn't think it would work having some work in the morning and some in the afternoon on the same job, but it did, and they were now an integral part of the work process. What would we do without them? Yet I realized the plant had produced without all of us before, and would continue after all of us were gone. And we would be gone someday; I assumed they knew that at the plant office, and this could be the reason that the engineer had pushed so hard to get his fence built. Rumors were usually persistent and started long before the action happened.

I had just gotten myself settled down to do the book work required to get the men paid for their work. The Soviets believe everything belongs to the working class. What a lie! The people have nothing, not even sufficient daily bread, and nothing belongs to them. If they owned anything, they would be capitalists. Actually, I had no claim either. Nothing was mine. It was not really my brigade, my men, my book work. I just called it that to make it apparent someone was responsible. We were all just numbers in that "big slave factory"—the paradise of the working class.

Downtown Engels Otto asked if I wanted to go with him to Engels. We had talked about it, but I never dreamed I would ever get the opportunity. For sure, I wanted to go. If the right soldier was on guard duty, he would let us out of the camp—Otto, the cultural event coordinator, and me, the Brigadier. I put the book work away, and was ready to leave immediately. I did not have to shave, take a shower, put on clean clothes, or comb my hair. There was nothing to comb—it was cut too short.

The guard waved us through the gate without asking any questions. We both were well known. Here we were outside, walking in the people's paradise "prison." We took the usual route toward the factory and followed the road straight toward Engels. What should we do? Walk around town, eat Russian food at a cafe, go to the movie theater? As we walked, there was nobody around. At the camp one had to be careful what one said and to whom. One never knew who was listening. I shared with Otto the thoughts I had just before he picked me up, and we continued talking about the concept. The Soviets made a big mistake letting us

WPs come into their country and look behind the facade, be in contact with the working class, and then let us go home. We are true ambassadors of the "Worker's Paradise."

"Hopefully, someone will listen to us about what we have heard and seen to make a difference before apathy sets in, and a generation arrives that does not want to hear about it anymore. Bellies full, we could settle into a 'normal' life again, and turn into belly-filled, don't-care-anymore civilians."

Otto laughed. He laughed more about the future outlook than for the ironic reality I had tried to develop.

"We will never forget. You are right, but the next generation will not listen anymore."

When we arrived in town, the first thing that caught my eye was that the street signs were in both German and Russian. The German signs were mounted above the Russian ones. Engels must have had a strong German influence. It was once the capital of the Volga-German district, with German schools and church services. I realized that they were now Russian, but they had kept their German traditions. As the babushka told me at that bazaar in front of the factory:

"If you go home, our husbands and sons will return."

That would be her hope to her grave. How much suffering was behind the windows of these homes! Not only in this city, but all over this country. Maybe a day will come, I thought, when the brutality and beastly treatment of the people of this great Russia will be known. Communism destroys nations, no matter how great they are! Socialism undermines the individual's initiative, to be forced to depend entirely on the government, which was the ruling class in the Soviet Socialist Republic.

"Souper" or Dinner A sign in front of a building indicated that it was a restaurant, a place to eat. When we went inside, it felt like "home"-railroad station waiting room third class — only the German soldiers were missing and the Red Cross nurses who gave out the barley soup. It was a fairly good-sized room with a high ceiling and plaster ornaments from a craftsman of times long gone; only a few lightbulbs working in a fixture that held many lights. The walls had not been painted since the day they were built — variations of faded gray blended with the dust and harmonized with the few lightbulbs, making the room rather monotonous. Wooden tables were surrounded by chairs of different styles in line with each other, and some separated, so the room did not appear so empty. One table was occupied by three men. They talked very loudly. At least it sounded loud since nobody else was in the room. Otto and I chose a table and sat down, anxious to see what would happen. A middle-aged woman came from somewhere behind us and asked only if we wanted to eat. "*Da*," we answered, and she disappeared. We joked that she would bring a menu and we would be able to read at least: soup, *kasha*, and *chai* (tea). Our waitress reappeared and served us soup. It was steaming hot and more solid than our servings in camp. We got the impression this place was a one-woman operation: waitress, cook, dishwasher, and cashier. She did not show any surprise that we spoke German. Either it was the custom in the old days and she knew our language, or she simply did not care. When we finished our soup I left my spoon on the china plate. I thought this was the first time I had eaten on a china plate since I left Berlin. No, it was the second time. The first was at Silvertooth's where we cut the firewood over in Saratov. How far back was that? The waitress came back and set two bowls of *kasha* in front of us.

This was our dinner "souper." The *kasha* was the same as we had in camp, only much more skillfully prepared: cooked in broth with oil and fat added. It was home cooking, and it tasted good. We laughed about not reading the menu so we could order and not knowing what we would have to eat until it was served.

Reminiscence During our meal I told Otto about the Russian restaurant in Berlin, close to the Ku'damm, that served *borscht* with all the ingredients and sour cream. I even jumped back to Paris where they had a Russian émigré restaurant with *balalaika* music — everything was authentic. I was full of memories of things long gone. Otto and I laughed as we talked, and I "forgot" we were in Engels in the third-class "waiting room" of a railroad station. Was it proper to tip in the Soviet Union? I slipped a ruble under my plate. I guess I felt sorry for the place. We went to a table close to the exit where she took our money and said "*Dasvidanye*" (good-bye). She had treated us like anybody else. That felt good. What must she have thought when she found that ruble? Did I scratch the system with my little toe?

Movie We walked the very poorly lit streets to the movie theater. It didn't matter what film was showing; we paid and went inside. There was no concession stand to buy candy, chocolate bars, or drinks. I told Otto about the popcorn they sell in American theaters. Here you could bring your own. The few people inside were talking and laughing, yelling to each other over the empty seats. The atmosphere was joyous, like a children's matinee in any town anyplace. The *kino* (movie theater) must have been a ballroom at one time. The floor was level, with wooden chairs that were comfortable if you sat on your folded coat. Lights went out and the film started flickering on the screen. When the actor's name or a beloved actress came on, the crowd responded with enthusiastic approval. The sound track was too loud, echoing off the bare walls. The movie took place on a *kolkhoz* (collective farm). The main actress was beautiful, with the gorgeous figure of a big-city girl. She was a tractor driver and fell in love with the best-looking coworker. She was sent to a tractor school and was so eager to learn she took another course. When she finally went back to the *kolkhoz*, her boyfriend was involved with another girl. She told him off and ran to her tractor, embraced it, and promised to always keep it in good running condition. There was applause from the women's side of the theater. Then the grand finale came on. All the actors marched arm-in-arm in a long row toward the camera, singing an enthusiastic song, and coming closer until the whole screen was filled with one beautiful face ornamented with grease spots that seemed to belong to a good lady tractor mechanic. The movie ended amid laughing, yelling, and teasing among the folks who enjoyed it as much as we did.

The Way Home We walked toward the camp, still talking and laughing about the "glorious" story the film portrayed. It was basically the same type of propaganda we received from the Nazis, just a bit more simple, designed for general audiences. As we approached the camp, we noticed someone was following us. We were surprised to discover it was the German camp commander. He seemed a little sheepish as he had not expected to meet us. Without a word came a silent agreement not to know about each other being outside. We reported back in at the camp gatehouse. The guard, laughing, asked if we had a good time, and with a grin on his face and a hand movement indicated something that would have been our last thought after three years as WPs. I assumed his demeanor was different for the commander. "Nichivo." What did I care? His opinion did not make me who I was.

I enjoyed being with those Russian civilians, but it was puzzling that no one was the least bit suspicious of us. Nobody even noticed us. Did a WP show up occasionally so that it was nothing new? If someone did recognize us as WPs, they must have seen us as any other beings. Did I have a smile on my face about the whole experience when I fell asleep!

Action and Reaction Fact seemed to follow the rumors. Without a rear-end inspection, Group III prisoners (our four-hour workers) were sent to camp one, the camp we arrived at three years before. Hermann Krauss was one of them. I gave him the address of Annemarie so he could write and tell her how well I had survived.

We were happy they were sending Group III home. Maybe it would come to an end for all of us soon. One thing I learned in Russia: One is never sure of anything until it happens, and then it is often different from what was promised. Nothing is sure until it is completely finished. The good-byes were hopeful, not emotional like in previous years when the first prisoners were sent home.

Our morning shift was hectic without the four-hour workers. Supervisors cursed and blamed me for allowing them to leave. Would the wagon factory collapse without them?

The *natchalniks* now saw what they had in those cheap four-hour laborers. They did not pay them fairly for their labor. Those poor guys were not able to earn even an extra piece of bread in four hours, and they were more in need of getting their strength back than the rest of us.

The system rewarded only the best workers. Everyone else was left behind. The best workers' names were put on a blackboard for everyone to see and admire, or to hate. They got the bonuses. The next worker who was just a little behind had to labor harder to beat number one, and have his name put on top. It is the plan for workers in this "Paradise of Socialism."

When a Russian wants to disgrace a person or situation, he curses and spits on him or it. That's what I would have liked to do to that system.

I had deep compassion for these Russians because I knew things would never change as long as they had their current leaders.

The *natchalniks* did not know how to adjust to the new situation. The Class III WPs had spoiled them, and now their men would have to work harder. The engineer must have been the only one who knew about the change before it happened, and he did not say anything to the *natchalniks*. He must have had orders from above and knew they could not be changed. Was that the reason he pushed so hard with fabricating the fence parts?

I remembered Goebbels' slogan that elevated Hitler's megalomania:

"*Führer befiel, wir folgen*" ("Our leader commands, and we will follow.")

The two systems and flags were similar. One was red with the golden hammer and sickle, and the other was the same red with a black swastika on a white circle. Some see only the gold in the Russian, others saw only the white spot in the German. But some saw only the red in both of them.

The workers in the plant survived somehow. What other choice did they have? We did our best, but the atmosphere changed for the worse. It was a difficult challenge.

I still enjoyed my moments with Misha in the tall grass. He continually reminded me to be sure when I got home, and went to America, to tell them how it really was in Russia.

"Tell them someone has to stand up to our elite upper class. We need help from the outside to change things here in Russia."

Misha acted like I was his only hope. What could I do? I didn't know, but I knew I would tell.

Exodus About six weeks later the news came that we were also to leave Engels and go back to Camp I. That was the camp with the beautiful flower gardens. We were rushed to get out that morning. We didn't even go to the factory. We packed our belongings, cleaned the quarters, and wondered who would occupy them next. I worried they might take my one new linen shirt when we got to the other camp, because we were not allowed more than what we wore.

They called us for the final count. Nobody would be left behind. We made a formation. We walked out in the same direction we walked every morning, and every noon, day after day. When we got to the road through the factory, Russians stood in hallways and alongside the buildings. We wondered if it was because we were leaving, or was it because their men would be closer to coming back? Misha, my Russian friend, waved at me and his eyes said for the last time:

"*Tell them.*"

I stepped out, shook his hand and gave him my new linen shirt. He had more need of it than I did.

A little over three years ago the Russians were our enemies, and now they were standing there waiting to see us walk out, and waving to us with tears in their eyes. It was a moving moment for all of us. A French saying came to mind, here of all places:

"*Partir c'est mourir un peu, mourir de ceux qui on aime. Partir c'est mourir un peu.*" ("To leave is a bit like dying, dying from those we love. To leave is a bit like dying.")

As we marched toward the usual boxcars, we met our camp replacements surrounded by many guards with their rifles ready to shoot at a moment's notice. Some had vicious dogs on short leashes. We had not seen anything like that since our march to Sagan in the first days of our captivity. The men, and women too, looked awful. Their clothes, torn and dirty, hung on their bodies. Most of them did not look up at us, but fixed their eyes on the ground. A few met our eyes as if to say, 'You go, we come.' They looked pitiful, Russian men and women dressed alike in pants, jackets, and overcoats. We must have given that same impression when we arrived in Atkarsk after having waited for two nights for the ride from Saratov. But many of these prisoners would never see freedom again. And they were imprisoned by their own people.

When we got to our boxcar, we hopped in and had ample room to spread out. I got excited the last time crossing the Volga, but this time even more so, going west. As the train rattled over the steel bridge, I looked down into the slow-moving water. I recalled the days sitting on the stairs to the upper room at the sawmill camp. We had come a long way since that first camp, and much had passed. The Volga still moves slowly toward the Caspian Sea. So it is with our lives, too. God's cycle of laws:

Nothing stands still. All is in a flow, leading to somewhere.

Was all this real? Had I walked over that river when it was frozen? Camp Engels? The factory, fighting with the *natchalniks*, pleasing some, never pleasing others. The fence construction? Hopefully someone will plant trees and bushes for the workers to enjoy in their paradise. And maybe they will get more to eat, and more of life's necessities? Oh, what we left behind us! Will the Russians ever experience a change during their lifetime? And the Volga continues to flow into the Caspian Sea. Misha, I will tell all who are willing to listen. Misha, I will tell them. I promise.

Camp I

Return to Where It Began We arrived in Saratov. A short walk to camp, and there we were right back where we started from, a little over three years before — 1945. Our first impression was that the camp had changed for the better. The flower gardens were even prettier than I remembered. The barracks were all above ground, solid and well built. The meals were by far better than any other place. The camp looked more like a resort, Russian style, than a WP camp. I met a few of the Group III men who left from Engels just a few weeks before. Most of them had already gone home. Hermann Krauss was among them. He could send good news to my wife Annemarie and Hans.

Brigadier "Nyet" Someone suggested that I be a brigadier again.

"*Nyet*, no more, I want to just do my work, and not be tied down with all that book work at night. I've done my share."

I managed to get assigned to a commando "transport" unit. The job was riding around working hard for a while loading or unloading, then riding again. The commando usually stayed out all day, and did not come in for noon break. That meant we would get lunch and dinner at once and filled the belly really full. We walked out with the regular brigade to a garage where most heavy trucks were overhauled and repaired. The garage was always in need of additional specialists and mechanics. Everyone went to his usual job except we five guys who waited to jump on a truck and go. Delay, delay — nobody seemed to know when we would leave. Finally a truck was assigned to us. The driver was cursing and cussing. He couldn't get the truck started. The motor was barely turning over. It was not getting enough electrical power.

Specialist Many years ago when I graduated from high school, I wanted to be an auto mechanic and worked on a volunteer basis in a garage for about four months. Seeing the inside of this profession, I decided there must be a cleaner way to make a living. No matter how clean I started out in the morning, I'd look like a grease monkey by evening. I did learn how motors worked, though.

The driver quit cursing and started kicking at the tires. As time dragged on, one of the guys was concerned we would lose our assignment and get a worse job. I looked inside the cab and found two batteries and a switch. One position was for both batteries to start the motor, and the other position was to charge the batteries one at a time. Some clever guy had worked it all out. I touched one of the battery cables. It was hot. A connection was not correct and current ran into this cable, not as a conductor but as a resistor to turn it into heat. I followed the cables to find out how they were wired originally. I got a wrench and changed a connection. I called the driver back and indicated he should try it again. He turned the key, pushed the starter, and *putt, putt, putt*, the motor burst into life.

"*Khorosho*," the chauffeur jumped at me. "Specialist, specialist."

I was afraid he would tell the boss and I would have to work in the garage. "Specialist, *nyet*."

I just figured it out. I pointed to my bent left arm to show the biceps muscle, "*Nyet*," and then pointed to my head, "*Da*."

I was trying to say in sign language, "Not with muscle power, but by using the head can one solve problems."

He thought I pointed to my head to indicate he was nuts. He lunged at me, but the other guys held him back, and explained what I had tried to say with my gestures. He caught on and laughed, and we shook hands. We drove quite a ways out of town where we found trenches, well built, but never used. Were they for the defense of Saratov? Maybe our troops never came that close to the city—German attacks concentrated on Stalingrad.

We did not find our location or what we came for. But what a pleasant drive in the surrounding country! Back at the garage the chauffeur made the same gesture as I had shown him that morning. He thought it was a great joke, and was still laughing when we met the others and walked back to camp. I never went back to that assignment.

Sawmill To make money, one would have to have a good-paying job and be in camp for more than a month. I'd wait and see what kind of jobs came up. A few days later I was assigned to a sawmill close to the camp. It was much smaller and more primitive than the one we had worked in before. Our job was to pull logs to the saw for cutting. There were four or us, medium strong. I figured if four guys pitched in on one command we could move about anything, and we had the help of a Russian universal too, *la lomb* (crowbar). Anything imaginable could be moved, straightened out, repaired, broken, or destroyed with that tool. We always tried to be ahead of what the saw could cut, so we could have a little break in between.

The logs were dumped off the delivery truck as fast as possible. They often interlocked with each other. The *lomb* came in handy for untangling them. As the days passed, we became a team and did our job well. None of us was after the production percentage. We were new in camp. One could take advantage of us. We didn't care.

Youth Leader Otto was disappointed I did not volunteer to be a brigadier. He did not want to see me idle, so he offered me, or rather begged me, to become leader of the WP youth group.

"What is that?" I said. "There are no youth here."

Kids sixteen and seventeen years old who were drafted at the end of the war were now men, almost twenty years old.

Russian politicians wanted to instruct the younger ones, so they would get enthusiastic about socialism. I agreed on two conditions: I would not have to go to any indoctrination class, and I would do my own program and account to no one. Otto was relieved. Now he could "report" that the youth were in good hands.

At the first meeting, four showed up. They were bored, had nothing else to do, and came out of curiosity. I wanted to bring them something they had not heard. We talked about our home life, the chances of going home. We encouraged each other to keep hoping. We had gone through all those difficult years and the worst was now over. They must have noticed I did not beat the propaganda drum. The next time we got together, a couple brought along buddies and we grew to seven. In our informal talks, I told them to keep their eyes open, take in everything.

"Let it sink in, deep down, so when you go home nobody will be able to fool you about socialism. You will be able to tell 'em you experienced it and know what it's like."

I told them that was the most valuable thing they could take back home. The years in the camp then would not be wasted. No one disagreed, and as I brought it up casually and often, they caught on. That alone was worth the effort. Otto mentioned one day that he knew I was doing a good job since the group was getting larger. I was not impressed by the numbers. It was fun just to talk with those young men about important things in our lives.

Out The four of us enjoyed working together on our assignment at the sawmill. We learned the trick of log rolling; we built a track of small limbs to roll the logs on rather than on the soft dirt. One day after we got back from noon break, one heavy log did not roll straight on our track. I tried to push it in the proper direction but slipped, and the end of the log ran over my left foot. I could feel the pinch, but we kept working. We had enough material at the saw, and took a smoke break. We sat there maybe fifteen minutes. When I tried to get up, my foot was so painful that I could not put any weight on it. The other three guys went on working, letting me rest. At quitting time I could not walk. Two of the guys helped me limp back to the camp, hopping on my right foot. Fortunately, the mill was not far from the camp. The guys took me straight to the infirmary where I waited for the Russian doctor. When office hours came I got in line and told her what had happened. She told me to pull each of my toes really hard. When I pulled my middle toe, the pain was intense. Her diagnosis was a middle-bone fracture of my left foot. *Davai*, hospital.

Joachim Brennecke, called Achim, who attended the youth meetings, helped me pack my few belongings. I remembered him from the Engels camp. He was excited:

"Hansarmin, this is your chance to go home."

At that time I was in too much pain to care. All I wanted was to lie down. The hospital was just one room inside the camp designed for short-term stays. The really sick people had either died or been sent home.

There were no double bunks, only single beds. They were placed apart from each other with white bedsheets and a covered pillow. How inviting! Every move was painful. I looked forward to the evening meal of soup and bread and then rest. The night was not so pleasant; every time I turned the pain woke me up.

The following day the doctor put a cast on my leg from my toes to just below the knee. It felt good. After the cast dried, I could even walk — not very well, but the pain was gone. I got a pair of crutches and was able to get around pretty well. There was nothing to do but rest and eat good food. It was like a sanitarium, a place of recovery.

Meeting Again It was a wonderful surprise to see Dr. Rued again. He was the surgeon who cut out my boil in Atkarsk. He was pale and had lost weight since I had seen him in Atkarsk in September 1947. It was now August 1948. Rued had suffered a heart attack, and it showed. He moved very slowly and had been sent to the hospital to recuperate. I too had changed over the past year. I was in much better shape than in those days. In Atkarsk I was down to ninety pounds, but now I was almost back to my normal weight. I felt good. Rued and I visited often, and he told me the Russians had finally sent most of the Group III prisoners home and had closed the big hospital. Our hope and optimism soared!

A Visitor Someone called me to come to the window, actually our "visiting room." There stood Edmund Cord — the master baker from Berlin — the man with the malaria attacks. We were the two who shared the mattress in the boxcar from Saratov to Atkarsk, the trip that took two nights and days to go fifty miles. "Edmund!" I said, a lump in my throat. My eyes got a little wetter than normal. There he was behind a fence about twenty feet from the window. He looked pale. I didn't remember him being a heavy-set man, but now he was carrying even less weight.

"How are you? How did you know I was here? How did you get to the camp? What have you been doing?"

The questions were the same on both sides.

"You know, Hansarmin, word spreads among prisoners. I just heard you were here."

Edmund was in another camp pretty far away. They baked their own bread. He mentioned it was hard work, no machines, everything was done by hand. Nothing in the bakery was organized and he developed a system for bread making.

Eventually he got part-time help and did not have to do all the work by himself. Edmund came to Camp I to see the dentist, having got a ride on a truck that picks up their food supplies. We did not have enough time to talk about all that was on our minds. He said he would be back soon. Edmund. I thought he went home a long time ago.

A week later Edmund was back. He used the excuse that he had to see the dentist again. This time I went out to the fence, so we would have a little more privacy while we talked. He had baked a miniature loaf of bread for me just like we had at home, only much smaller. It was about six inches long, two inches wide, and two inches high — real crusty on the outside. Edmund had not forgotten our talks in the hospital about the good German bread with the crust on the outside.

The standard Russian bread tastes good — made from dark flour, but not baked. It's cooked in a square form and when fresh is quite moist. The bakers have to produce so many pounds of baked bread from so many pounds of flour. Since flour always falls to the side, the weight has to be made up with additional water so the moisture is still in the bread at delivery. It's a tricky process.

Edmund was all smiles when he saw my delight at the bread he had baked for me. I told him in a few words what had happened to me.

"Hansarmin, that leg in the cast will take you home."

Edmund seemed not so happy. The baker's job must have been a real burden to him. I thanked him again and encouraged him to keep his hopes up. He left, and I never saw him again.

Buttocks Parade Rumors were spreading. A committee was coming to sort us out. The day arrived, and the patients from the hospital lined up in the doctor's room: shirts off, give your name and sickness, drop your long johns, and turn around to show your rear end. The doctors and officers sitting in a half circle judged what was offered. I completed the turn on my crutches, and reached down a bit awkwardly for my long johns. The Russian officer sitting closest to me bent over to help me get my underwear. His gesture of help gave me hope that I might have won. A couple of days later a few of the patients' papers came back. Mine did not return. We found out those committees had a new way to sort out patients. Those prisoners who were not strong enough would be kept back. Maybe there had been too many casualties on the home-going trips. At any rate, the stronger of the weak ones had a better chance of going home. How things had changed since the beginning!

Achim found a walking stick for me. He figured they would not let me leave on crutches, so I started practicing walking with the cane. Achim was concerned about me and looked after my well-being. A doctor came one afternoon and wanted to see how I could walk without crutches. That was all. Was I on the way home? Achim mentioned he had "obtained" a uniform in good condition. He had planned that I should take this outfit: pants, jacket and army coat, and take them to his parents when I made it home. I was surprised a German uniform in such good condition still existed. Achim would try to get another uniform to take home when his time came. He procured a handmade, wooden suitcase to pack the things in. I gave Achim my last rubles. I would not need them anymore since rubles were not allowed out of the country. They had no value anyway outside the USSR. I practiced walking with the cane in one hand and the not-too-heavy suitcase in the other. The day finally came for us to leave. I wanted the cast removed since it would hinder my getting in and out of the boxcar, but Rued said:

"Hansarmin, leave it on until the last minute you walk out of here. You came back once before."

He hadn't forgotten. Our departure was cancelled — the boxcars did not come. Disappointment? Yes, but our papers did not come back, so there was still a chance.

A Family Picture The next day when the mail came I had a postcard with a picture of Annemarie and Hans sewn in the corner. I had asked so often for a picture. Others had received them, so we knew they were allowed through. Here was mine. They both looked great. Hans was a first grader. He had started to school at Easter time. That picture was such a gift, and it made up for our delayed departure.

Two days later was **THE DAY**. Achim came with the news that the boxcars were there and had plenty of straw inside for us to lie on. They had already loaded our food supply. He reported everything that happened, except what the menu would be. The call came for us to come out to the cars. "Now," Rued said, "let me take off your cast." It took him about a minute to get rid of it. I walked for the first time since the accident with both feet on the ground. It hurt, but not as much as before. Rued teasingly said there never was a fracture. Dr. Rued did not make it this time. He had to be in better physical condition. We walked through the camp and out a side gate that led directly to the tracks. Some of the fellows were standing along the way waving us on. Achim was there, too, wishing us a safe and speedy return home. Even some of the youth group waved. I said "good-bye" to all my friends left behind. Four big Russian boxcars waited for us at the same spot where we had arrived three and a half years before.

"Saratov" Camp I, departure date: September 1948!

Going West

First Class: Straw Bedding and Doors Open A sympathetic Russian captain greeted us with a smile: "*Damoi*." (Going home.) The guards, young soldiers, seemed to be excited about this trip through a part of their vast country, or was it being released from boring barracks duties? We chose how we wanted to be grouped together and climbed into our cars. First class! The floor was covered with a thick layer of straw. I was spoiled now. I had not slept on hard, wooden planks since the trip from Breslau to Saratov — nor even on that ill-fated trip from the hospital in Saratov to Atkarsk. I carried a mattress on which Edmund and I laid comfortably. The mattress on my last hospital bed was also very comfortable. The guards said the sliding boxcar doors would stay open. We would travel through the Russian countryside and see things, not be spirited along in locked cattle cars. As we settled down, the switcher came to connect our cars to a waiting freight train.

I heard whistles at this railroad yard that sounded like the tugboats and ferries in New York Harbor. How far back was all that?

Our train moved slowly, pulling out of the yard, passing the suburbs of Saratov, and traveling through the countryside. Twilight came and soon it was dark. We closed the doors ourselves to keep out the cold night air. The clickety-click of the rolling wheels was a soothing sound, especially with the assurance we were traveling west, going home. I fell into a restful sleep.

Halt We traveled for two days, and Achim's wooden suitcase came in handy either as a table on which to eat or as a stool to sit on. We did not talk much. Each of us hung onto his own thoughts and hopes about what the homecoming would be like — how things will have changed. Little children had grown up a bit, and we were not the same. We had changed also.

For the past hour or so the train had been rolling slower, like running on a track in repair. It pulled onto a sidetrack and came to a halt. Maybe some fast-moving train had to pass us. Soon the guards came and told us we could get out as this would be a long stop. It felt good to walk around and to meet and talk to the guys from the other cars. It was like a sightseeing trip. Word spread that the engine had broken down, and there was no spare engine available. They sent for parts for the engine to be repaired where it stood.

There was no place to go, no village, just open country. Our destination was Brest, on the border between Russia and Poland, and here we were stuck about one-third of the way there. The following days our rations were shortened. We had only enough food for the trip without the delay, and it had to be rationed now to make it last to the end of our journey. A scary thought crossed our minds: Would the Russian captain deliver us to another camp before we ran out of food? We would be "newcomers," starting at the bottom of the totem pole with the last chance of being sent home. But the wheels started rolling again after being stranded for over four days. This interruption of our travels dampened our spirits. Everyone's thought was, "Will the repaired engine get us home?" That the rations were shorter than "normal" was okay — we were used to that.

Final End of the Wide Track We arrived fairly late in the evening in Brest. Our captain in charge arranged for us to get hot, solid soup, more than we had ever gotten at any meal. And "for dessert," a shower with plenty of hot water and soap, and the first effective delousing. We could hardly catch our breath. The next day the train for Frankfurt an der Oder was scheduled to leave. Would we be on it? There was a train on the European track waiting, and we saw them load the food supply. The past years of waiting turned into a state of being ready any minute for any move. I did not sleep that night. It was hard to comprehend that all of us assembled here were on our way home.

The next morning we got a bowl of good, hot soup, which made up for the shortcomings during our trip thus far.

Was all this behind us? Forgotten? Everything had changed so fast. The morning hours passed with us listening to the rumors spreading around. No one had to give us orders. We were ready and in the right place at the right time to get on the right train. The boxcars were the smaller German type, and they would be going west. Every one of us was geared in only one direction. We did not know what lay before us, but we knew what we left behind. All of us took something home in our minds, and would talk about it if anyone was willing to listen.

An order was given. We got in line, were counted, and divided into those waiting cars. Nobody called our names anymore. We were just numbers now that filled the train. There were no more Russian guards. It was over! We were in the cars, ready to roll west. The whole process was well organized and did not take long. The train pulled out of the camp, doors open.

At the first stop, word spread from the kitchen wagon: "Come and get it!" Two guys from each car went to the kitchen car and returned with a bucket full of solid stew. Every four to six hours, wherever it fit into a stop, the call came from the rear: "Come and get it!" Every time it was a solid meal. It seemed like they wanted to fatten us up on this last trip and dull our memories of all those lean years.

Partir C'est Mourir un Peu My thoughts went back to those left behind. Edmund, in charge of the bakery. He was so sad at our last visit. Achim, always with a smile that helped him get through. The others in the camp, in the hospital.

Dr. Rued, get your strength back so you can come home. Be strengthened in your hope that we made it.

The Russian workers in the factory did the same thing day in and day out with no hope for a change and a future. They were prisoners in their own country.

"Misha, my Russian friend, yes, I will tell them. Wherever I have a chance, I will tell them. You must not give up hope."

I was on the way home, full of hope, plans, full of expectation to begin a new life with my wife and son. A new existence. It will be different now. Hitler is gone. Yes, a new life. And above all, the desire and hope to go to the United States. My intuition cautioned me: Wait, Hansarmin, wait, take it step by step, go home and see what's there.

I knew I was getting ahead of myself. But I knew what I wanted. This time nothing would hinder me. Stop, wait a second, Hansarmin. Didn't I figure out how to get home by not gaining any weight, and did it work? What was the word that came as a comforter:

"In the fullness of time."

And I am in better condition than I was a year ago:

"Father, Thy will be done!"

On one of the stops along the way, we got out of the cars to do the necessities. There were plenty of open fields. The railroad personnel were German. We grouped around them and bombarded them with questions: How is it at home? What is a blockade? What does it mean that Berlin is divided into sectors? They had one answer for each question: "You will see." The two railroaders gave us not one little hint. Why didn't they talk? Didn't they trust each other because they lived in different parts of Berlin? "You will see" was the stoic answer. Something must be really wrong to make them not talk. The only thing we found out was the Oder River was the border between Germany and Poland, and that Frankfurt an der Oder was on the German side.

Bells Are Ringing We came to a large city. One of the men said it was Frankfurt an der Oder. But we had not crossed the Oder River, so we must have still been on the Polish side. Our train came to a stop in the railroad yard. In the not-too-far distance we saw the silhouette of Frankfurt! It must have been late afternoon. It was so quiet. No rattling of the rail wheels, not much activity in the railroad yard, and not much talking either. Everyone just hung onto his own thoughts. Suddenly the bells of the churches in Frankfurt across the river started ringing. It must be Sunday. "Sunday?" We knew only "*Vikbodnoi*"—shift change day or a day off. "*Vikbodnoi*" was on a different day of the week for every factory.

The sound of those beautiful bells brought tears to our eyes. This was coming home!

In our boxcar it was quieter than before. Nobody wanted to interrupt the silence. The train moved slowly on, and soon we had crossed over the Oder bridge to the German side. This was the Oder, not "my" Volga. It was good coming home!

It was German soil we stepped on as we got out of the cars. The first thing we saw in our new German camp was a complex of barracks. We were divided according to the regions of our homes. My barracks was the assembling place for Berliners. I did not know any of the men, but being from the same hometown, we buddied up quickly.

The trip to Berlin would begin on Monday morning. After a shower and shave and new shirts and underwear, we registered to get the official release document for our prisoner-of-war time. Later came an official who was assigned to take us to Berlin. He acted like a party worker with some kind of socialistic background. He was the type I would not trust — cold, impersonal. Whatever he said had no heart or even any friendliness. I never saw him smile. He seemed very unhappy — unhappy because of his job assignment? Maybe he thought he was called to do something better? Or was it too routine to bring prisoners from Frankfurt to Berlin? Maybe he had a miserable family life, or did he have a family? I did not dare ask. He was the type who did his job to please somebody above, not for the joy of doing a given task well. He encouraged us to give our names and addresses. They would be announced over Berlin radio so our families would know we had come home. I did not want to give my name for fear that someday someone from the party would knock on my door. I did not want to have anything to do with them. As we listened to Radio Berlin, we detected left-wing propaganda in every announcement. During the broadcast, the announcer read the names of everyone in our room except mine. The other fellows tried to persuade me that it was okay, that my family would know I had come home. Finally I gave in. The man had waited patiently for me. He knew how many people had reported to him, and that I alone was left. That gave me some compassion for him. As I came back from the washroom, he greeted me and the others with a big "Halloh." They had just announced my name and address over the radio. That last night it was hard to sleep. I wondered what I would find in Berlin. What was waiting for us? Suddenly I was fully conscious. That inner voice again:

"It will be in *the fullness of time* after this one last night."

I fell sound asleep.

We got up early the next morning. We had to catch a train that ran on a tight timetable. It would not wait for us. We had no soup for breakfast that day, only a slice of bread and a cup of hot black water; that was coffee? Our guide took us to the railroad station. He assured us that a car was reserved for the *Heimkehrer* (homecomers) and it would be the last one on the train. We were not to get into the cars occupied by other travelers. He was quite serious. It sounded almost like we had leprosy, and should not come into contact with other human beings.

I was surprised how well I could walk. I had to get used to stepping down on my foot after five weeks in a cast, without using my cane. I became aware that I was in good physical condition.

Our train came, the Frankfurt-Berlin German Railway line. The cars had seats. No more boxcars. No more lying on the floor. Our reserved car, the last one, had no glass in any of the windows. It was completely air-conditioned. The air blew right through. The man in charge was embarrassed. He could not understand why someone put a car in that condition on the train specially requested for released prisoners of war. I felt sorry for him.

I speculated that maybe a former prisoner of war had picked that particular car so no one could ride in it. The *Heimkehrer* would have to mingle with the civilians in the other cars. I grinned at the thought.

We hopped into the next car and sat right next to the German travelers. We did not have to tell them where we had come from. They realized who we were by the things we asked about. We never got a straight answer. Different words, always the same thoughts, "Come home and you will see."

We arrived at Berlin-Schlesischer Bahnhof and were invited into the waiting room of the station where we each got an apple and a slice of bread with some lard smeared over it. A few of the men's wives were at the station. The radio announcement from the night before had gotten through. We sat around a table, introduced ourselves, and listened to what those women said about the situation in Berlin.

We finally understood that Berlin had been divided into four sectors. One was East Berlin occupied by the Russians. That was our arrival pint, as East Germany completely surrounded the city of Berlin. Berlin was like an island surrounded by the Communist-Russian-occupied East German State. The western part of the city made up the other three sectors: American, British, and French, and formed one unit. The socialistic government of East Berlin had cut the electricity to West Berlin in an attempt to get the western powers out of the city. The three western governments decided to supply Berlin by air. That is what they now call the Luftbruecke — the Berlin Airlift. What a task — what a challenge! It had been in operation for six months and was working well.

As we sat there and listened, the door to the waiting room opened and my mother stood there, hesitating before entering and looking around. With one jump I was at the door holding her in my arms — no words, just holding. I had not expected anyone would come here to greet me. It was too much. I let all my emotions go and tears streamed down my cheeks. We both cried as I led my mother to the table and introduced her to the others.

My first question was:

"How did you know I had arrived?"

The main electric plant for Berlin was in the eastern part of the city. By order of the Russians, East Berlin stopped the power supply to the West. To survive in West Berlin, the city was obliged to crank up the old (fifty years and older) power stations to supply power for industry and streetcar service. There was not enough energy for households. By dividing the western part of Berlin into different sections, households got electricity two hours during the day and two hours at night. The timetable rotated to give everyone better and worse times of electrical power. My homecoming was announced on the news at 10:00 P.M. At that time there was no power in my mother's apartment. A lady in Wilmersdorf, a district next to Friedenau where we lived, heard the news, forgot the name, but remembered the address, Sued-West-Corso 2, and went over the next morning to ask the concierge if anyone was expecting a prisoner of war to come home.

"That must be Mr. Schuetz," the concierge decided.

The lady talked with my mother over the intercom, and told her someone at Sued-West-Corso 2 would be coming home from a Russian prisoner of war camp and would arrive at 10:00 A.M. at the Schlesischer Bahnhof. My mother got all excited, but wanted to be sure it was really me. A young MD and his wife lived in our apartment and had the privilege of having a telephone. The doctor called the radio station and found it really was Hansarmin Schuetz who would be at Schlesischer Bahnhof the next morning. My mother called some friends who would get the message to my mother-in-law, not knowing if Annemarie and Hans were still in Berlin, or if they had returned to Stotternheim in the Russian-occupied German zone in Thuringia on Sunday, where she had a job as a kindergarten supervisor during the war. We rushed out and drove the S-Bahn to Charlottenburg where my mother-in-law lived.

When Annemarie got the message that I had returned, it was too late for her to make it to the railroad station in the east sector. She decided to wait for me at home. She, Hans, my mother-in-law, and a friend waited patiently for me to ring the doorbell. How wonderful she looked! Just like the picture I had received three days before my departure from Saratov. And our son, then six and a half years old, a schoolboy, stood bravely by the side of his mother waiting for a father he had heard so much about to come home.

There was much hugging and embracing. I was home!

I brought Hans a present from the long journey of nineteen days from Saratov to Berlin. It was the apple I had received just that morning from the Railroad Station Mission. That was all that I was allowed to bring.

Annemarie and Hans should have returned to Stotternheim but for some reason, she had delayed it one more day, and on that day I arrived home.

In the hallway of the apartment hung my grey flannel suit, just waiting for me to put it on. After a shower and dressing in my own suit, I had to explain the signet ring on my left hand. I told them about Egon von Rège, who was sent home two years before my time, and his ring was here safe with me. Tomorrow I would send it by registered mail to return it to the true owner, living in Hamburg.

Annemarie and Hans had to return to Thuringia to prepare for the move.

After a couple of short visits to Berlin, two months later we took up residence in the apartment with my mother.

I had a physical checkup and an X-ray taken of my foot. The doctor asked me what had been wrong with my foot. I told him about the middle-bone fracture about seven weeks ago in Russia.

"We turned your X-ray upside down, but there was no indication of a fracture. It could have been a pinched nerve that caused the pain, but with the cast and the rest, it healed. You are in good shape."

I remembered the "voice" that came to me in September 1947 when I was called back from the trip:

"In the fullness of time, no matter in what condition you are, you will go home."

The year before I arrived Germany had a hard winter, and there was barely enough food for those at home. My whole family had experienced the fulfillment of God's promise of my healthy return after three and one-half years as a prisoner of war in Russia (April 22, 1945–October 11, 1948).

Epilogue

Franz Gielen, the first *Heimkehrer*, brought the word of my well-being to my mother-in-law. In November 1945, Annemarie received the good news of my whereabouts and that I was alive and well. Rudi Strohbach, the one who collected all the recipes, visited in Berlin and brought a more up-to-date report.

I delivered the "good" uniform to Achim Brennecke's parents and told them to expect a man to come home, not the boy who left years before. Achim came home almost a year later, safe and sound.

The master baker from Berlin, Edmund Cord, who suffered from malaria attacks, made it home six months after my return. Edmund lived in the Russian sector and my home was fortunately in the American sector of Berlin. Since the blockade of West Berlin, all supplies to the city came by airlift. Coal was a very rare item, but Edmund managed to get some to us for heating our rooms.

We had many pleasant visits from the now MD, Dr. Günther Goebel, our "doctor" in the sawmill camp. He enjoyed our two sons. Our second son, Michael, was born in 1950.

Through a dear friend from the army service in Munich, Erwin Reddig, who worked for the CIA in Tempelhof Airfield during the airlift, I got my first job in December 1948 as a jeep driver for the A&A Communication Services at the Tempelhof Airport. The good food from the mess hall got me back to my normal weight and strength quickly.

Since I was born in Bromberg (West Prussia — now Bydgoszcz), a part of Germany that was ceded to Poland at the peace treaty of 1918, I was classified as a displaced person. My wife was born in Bolivia, so it took us almost three years to receive emigration visas to the U.S.A. Before we sailed from Hamburg in November 1951, we had a pleasant farewell visit with Egon von Rège and his lovely wife. Egon proudly wore his signet ring that I had returned to him on the finger of his left hand. In December 1951 we arrived in beautiful Colorado Springs, Colorado, our HOME ever since.

After more than forty years, we took a trip to Germany and had a very pleasant visit with Hermann Krauss and his dear wife in his hometown of Güglingen. Hermann was the schoolteacher, organist, and philosopher. We were together in the camp at the wagon factory in Engels. After his release, he wrote articles for local newspapers about his experiences in Russia.

****

"I have made big mistakes. I am filled with deadly horror. I feel I am lost in an ocean of blood. The blood of countless victims. It is beyond the point of no return. To save our homeland, Russia, it would take ten men like Francis of Assisi."
—Some of the last words of Vladimir Ilich Ulyanov (Lenin) before his death.

"The German people are not worthy that I should be their Führer."
—The last remarks of Adolf Hitler before his death.

"Therefore I say unto you, take no thought of your life, what ye shall eat, or what ye shall drink; nor yet for your body, what ye shall put on. Is not life more than meat, and the body more than raiment? Behold the fowls of the air, for they sow not, neither do they reap, nor gather into barns, yet your heavenly Father feeds them. Are ye not much better than they?"
—Matthew 6:25–26 (KJV)

Looking back to the situations I had to experience, I see God's hand in every happening. God directed me in preparation for receiving His grace in the fullest meaning. It happened in 1955, here in Colorado Springs at the then new headquarters of the Navigators, in the dingy little office of Lorne Sanny, who was the vice president of the Navigators at that time. Introduced through Peter Schneider, trainee at the Navigators and a former U-boat officer living in Berlin, I accepted the Lord Jesus Christ as my personal Savior and Lord.

Over the years, God provided guidance through many people to prepare the way to where I stand today. Jim Rayburn, founder of Young Life, was my Sunday School teacher for many years. Corrie Ten Boom, the Dutch woman who lost her family in the Nazi concentration camps, for helping and hiding Jewish families from the Gestapo during the occupation of Holland by the Nazis. During her worldwide traveling, spoke many times in Colorado Springs about the full awareness of the indwelling of the Holy Spirit in the believer. Today I am grateful for the guidance God has provided to experience the true meaning of letting God's Word speak to me. And it speaks according to my needs.

How beautifully Paul expresses this in Romans 8:28: "And we know that all things work together for good to them that love God, to them who are the called according to His purpose."

Glossary

(German and Russian words used in the text)

Aufstehen	G	Get up, stand up
Babushka	R	Grandmotherly woman
Bafeika	R	Long ski parka
Balalaika	R	Russian stringed instrument
Bald	G	Soon (shortly)
Banja	R	Bath
Befohlen (God....)	G	God be with you
Bistro	R	Faster
Bleiben	G	Remain; stay
Bolshoi	R	Large; great (Bolshoi Theater)
Borscht	R	Rich vegetable (beets) and meat soup topped with sour cream
Budit	R	It will be
Capusta	R	Sauerkraut
Chai	R	Tea
Chisty	R	Clean
Da	R	Yes
Damoi	R	Homeward
Dasvidanye	R	Good-bye
Davai	R	Let's ... (to) give
Einsatz	G	Deployment
Elektrishka	R	Streetcar
Fritz	R	Nickname for a German
Führer	G	Leader; Hitler's self-proclaimed title for himself
Gott	G	God
Guten Morgen	G	Good morning
Haus	G	House

Heimkehrer	G	The homecoming soldier
Humpel	G	Nickname for someone who limps
Kaputt	G	Broken; no longer works; finished, defeated, destroyed
Kasha	R	A mash of any grain food; cereal; potatoes
Khorosho	R	Good; well done
Kino	R	Movie theater
Kissly	R	Kind of half evaporated milk simmered for days on the kitchen stove
Kolkhoz	R	Collective farm
Komrad	R	Buddy; friend (also: fellow Communist)
Kraut	G	Cabbage
Landser	G	German soldier
Lomb	R	Crowbar
Magazine	R	Supply house
Magda	R	Woman; girl
Makhorka	R	Coarse-cut stems of the tobacco plant
Malinki	R	Little one; small (child)
Markenfrei	R	Meal with ration coupons
Nach	G	After, to, according to
Naryad	R	Document to show work performance (percent and pay)
Natchalnik	R	Boss, in charge of a department
Nichivo	R	I don't care; it doesn't matter
Nix	G	No; none; no more (from nichts: nothing)
Nix cultura	G/R	Bad behavior; no culture
Nyet	R	No; not
Papirosi	R	Cigarette with long cardboard mouthpiece
Piroshki	R	Small pastry filled with meat, cottage cheese, or cabbage
Prassnik	R	Special treat
Raz Dva Vzyali	R	One, two, together (in a singing rhythm to let a team pull at the same moment)
Reich	G	Realm (kingdom); the German Empire
Ritterkreuz	G	A military medal *pour le mérite* (for merit)
Robota	R	Work
Schnaps	G	Any hard liquor
Skoro	R	Soon
Spasibo	R	Thank you; thanks
Starchi	R	Man in charge
Stoy	R	Stop
Talon	R	Check for a meal or other products
Tsap-Tsarap	R	Stealing

Glossary

Unterarzt	G	Lieutenant
Uri	G	Watch
Vaterland	G	Fatherland
Vedro	R	Bucket
Vikbodnoi	R	Day off; shift-change day
Vojeno pleny — WP	R	Prisoner of war; POW; PW
Voyna	R	War
Wiese	G	Meadow
Yest	R	It is
Zaklyuchony	R	Russian civilian prisoners; hard-labor camp; gulag
Zakurim	R	Smoking; have a smoke

Index

Alps 38
Atkarsk 101, 104, 140, 151, 154
Austria 2, 3

Babelberg Studios 112
Balkan States 3
Bavaria 63
Berlin, Germany 1, 3, 6, 18, 36, 37, 39, 58, 59, 67, 79, 82, 83, 84, 112, 113, 144, 157, 160, 162
Berlin-Schlesischer, Bahnhof 158
Bert (escaped prisoner) 87
Black Sea 131
Bohemia 63
Bolivia 161
Brandenburg Gate 59
Brazil 113
Brennecke, Joachim 151, 152, 153, 161
Breslau 31, 141, 154
Brest, Belarus 155
Bromberg (Bydgoszcz), Poland 161
Bruno 84, 85, 86
Budapest, Hungary 64
Burmeister, Colonel 36
Buttocks parade 59, 77, 152

Camp I 43, 44, 148
Caspian Sea 96, 147
Caucasus Mountains 38, 42
Caucasus region 35, 38, 39
Chamberlain, Joseph 2
Charkov (Kharkov), Ukraine 22
Charlottenburg, Germany 41
Claudius, Matthias 124, 141
Colorado Springs, Colorado 161, 162

Copenhagen, Denmark 58
Cord, Edmund 100, 102, 103, 104, 105, 106, 151, 152, 161
Czechoslovakia 2, 3

Denmark 3, 113, 114
Don River 35
Dorpat (Tartu), Estonia 82
Dortmund, Germany 123
Düsseldorf, Germany 11, 12, 23, 43

Elbe River 3
Else, Tante 28, 49
Erfurt, Germany 12
Erich (head barber) 79
Estonia 82

Field hospital, Russian 22
Flying Hamburger (train) 113
France 2
Frankfurt an der Oder 155, 156
Frankfurter Zeitung (business paper) 113
Franklin School (Düsseldorf) 11
Friedenau 159
Fuhlbruegge, Otto 123, 124, 126, 127, 129, 131, 134, 142, 143, 144, 150

German Army Movie Outfit 35
Germany 3, 6
Gielen, Franz 33, 49, 59, 60, 77, 161
Goebbels, Joseph 2, 41, 146
Goebel, Günther 50, 55, 63, 64, 67, 68, 75, 95, 97, 98, 161

Index

Göring, Hermann 2
Great Britain 2
Gruendgens, Gustaf 112
Güglingen 161

Hamburg, Germany 59, 159, 161
Hamburg, S.S. 89, 113
Harold 64, 65, 66, 69, 71, 72
Hege, Franz 120
Hesse, Hermann 58
Hindenburg, Paul von 2
Hitler, Adolf 2, 3, 4, 18, 19, 25, 26, 41, 58, 59, 113, 114, 135, 136, 146, 162
Humpel (storekeeper) 63

International Red Cross 67

Joy (Russian woman) 69, 72

Kalmuck Steppe 36
Kara Sea 131
Karl 64, 65, 66, 69
Kaspek 38
Krauss, Hermann 124, 126, 145, 148, 161

Lemberg (LVOV), Ukraine 25
Luftbruecke (Berlin Airlift) 158
Luther, Martin 113

Magda (female guard) 62
Mein Kampf (Hitler) 2, 4
Misha (Russian overseer) 136, 137, 139, 140, 146, 147, 156
Moscow 19, 122, 134
Munich 18, 58, 79, 161

Nazi Party 2
Netherlands 3
New York, New York 58
Normandy 25
Norway 3

Oder River 34, 156, 157

Paris, Peter 40
Paris, France 40
P'atigorsk 38
Paul (welder) 99, 100, 139
Poland 3, 50, 59, 155, 156
Potsdam Radio Communications Barracks 6
"Prisoner Special" (streetcar) 44
Pushkin, Aleksandr Sergeyevich 119, 135

Rausch, Willi 120, 132, 133
Rayburn, Jim 162
Reddig, Erwin 161
Rhine River 2
Rued, Dr. 109, 112, 151, 153, 156
Russia 26, 34, 35, 37, 47, 51, 155, 160
Russian Half Moon 67

Saalfeld, Germany 60
Sagan (Zagan), Poland 24, 26, 49
Saratov (Zorotov), Russia 43, 44, 46, 62, 75, 99, 118, 148, 149, 151, 154, 159
Schmahl, Colonel 35, 36, 37, 38, 40, 41
Schneider, Peter 162
Schuetz, Annemarie 12, 23, 57, 58, 67, 148, 159, 161
Schuetz, Hans 12, 23, 57, 58, 109, 116, 148, 159
Schuetz, Michael Manfred 161
Schütz, Waldemar 22, 28, 43, 50, 84, 89
Schütz, Walther 11, 12, 43, 44
Siberia 118
Siddhartha (Hesse) 58
Silvertooth (factory boss) 64, 65, 66, 104
Stahnsdorf 6, 43, 60
Stalin, Joseph 19, 135, 137
Stalingrad (Volgograd), Russia 35, 43, 46
Stockholm, Sweden 58
Stotternheim 12
Strohbach, Rudi 33, 49, 60, 77, 161
Sweden 1, 89
Switzerland 1, 38, 89

Tank Officer Training School 41
Tchaikovsky, Pyotr Ilich 79

Index

Ten Boom, Corrie 162
Terek River 35, 39
13th Tank Division 35
Thuringia, Germany 23, 60, 67, 84

Ulyanov, Bladimir Ilich (Lenin) 119, 162
Ural Mountains 96, 118

Valkyrie 111, 115, 116
Vaterland 7, 9, 11

Volga River 34, 43, 47, 58, 75, 89, 90, 91, 96, 118, 119, 129, 130, 131, 147, 157
von Rège, Egon 91, 92, 95–96, 98, 159, 161

Wehrmachtsbericht 36
Wisent, Dr. 108, 112

Young Life 162